The Art of Unarmed Stage Combat

The Art of Unarmed Stage Combat is your guide to the principles and techniques of theatrical violence, combining detailed discussions of the mechanics of stage fighting with the nuances of acting decisions to make fighting styles reflect character and story. Fight director Robert Najarian offers never-before-published games and exercises that will allow you to develop the skills and concepts for performing violence for stage and screen. This title utilizes a unique system of training techniques that result in stage violence that is both physically engaging for you as a performer, while remaining viscerally engaging for the audience.

- Step-by-step illustrations and a fully integrated companion website with video examples of the techniques described in the book allow for easy and precise practice.
- Integration of performance and physical techniques gives you the skills to make the violence between characters look *and* feel realistic.
- From partnered warm-up exercises, to skill-building games, through stage combat techniques, this title gives you start-to-finish instruction.

Robert Najarian is an actor, instructor, and fight director hailing from the East Coast, currently an Assistant Professor of Theatre at the University of Michigan, Ann Arbor. He has taught at movement and stage combat workshops, such as the National Stage Combat Workshop at North Carolina School of the Arts, The Winter Wonderland Workshop in Chicago, IL, and The Paddy Crean Workshop at the Banff Center in Alberta, Canada. As a fight director, Najarian has staged the violence for more than 100 productions for stage and film. Fight direction credits include *Carmen* and *Macbeth* with Boston Lyric Opera, *As You Like It* with Commonwealth Shakespeare Company, *Don Quixote* with Boston Ballet, *Johnny Baseball* with American Repertory Theatre, *The Lieutenant of Inishmore* and *The Kite Runner* with New Repertory Theatre, and *She Kills Monsters* with Company One. Najarian is a Fight Director and Certified Teacher with the Society of American Fight Directors and a member of the Actors' Equity Association and SAG-AFTRA.

The Art of Unarmed Stage Combat

Robert Najarian

Focal Press
Taylor & Francis Group

NEW YORK AND LONDON

First published 2016
by Focal Press
711 Third Avenue, New York, NY 10017

and by Focal Press
2 Park Square, Milton Park, Abingdon, Oxon OX14 4RN

Focal Press is an imprint of the Taylor & Francis Group, an informa business

Library of Congress Cataloging in Publication Data
The art of unarmed stage combat/Robert Najarian.
　pages cm
　Includes index.
　1. Stage combat. I. Title.
　PN2071.F5N35 2016
　792.02′8 – dc23
　2015018090

ISBN: 978-1-138-93801-4 (hbk)
ISBN: 978-0-415-74249-8 (pbk)
ISBN: 978-1-315-81457-5 (ebk)

Typeset in Times New Roman and Helvetica
by Florence Production Ltd, Stoodleigh, Devon, UK

MIX
Paper from
responsible sources
FSC® C014174

Printed and bound in the United States of America by Sheridan Books, Inc. (a Sheridan Group Company).

To the memory of my mother and father,
Marla and Varant, who always knew
how to tell a story with life, humor, and
a good turn-of-phrase.

Contents

PART IV:
PROCESS AND PERFORMANCE   115

For instructional videos, please visit the companion website at www.focalpress.com/cw/najarian or by scanning the following code:

Acknowledgments

Time flows swiftly but never in the direction you think it will. And so it is that at the end I find myself at the beginning. It seems not long ago that I started writing down the techniques and precepts that I have been espousing in classes for over 10 years in these pages. But here they are. The raw material that is contained in these pages is nothing of my own. I have had the good fortune to be colleagues and friends with the best and brightest in this art. The generosity of spirit among performers, especially those who also share a particular interest in making stage combat an integral part of their artistic lives, allows dialogue and the sharing of ideas to exist. This book is only one example of the results of such collaboration within a society of artists.

First and foremost I must thank my two primary instructors, mentors, and friends Brad Waller and Robert Walsh who are both artists and human beings of the highest order. Without their guidance and friendship I would not have been able to realize what marvelous power the theatre can hold. To my close friend and colleague John Edward "Ted" Hewlett I owe more than I can ever say for being the other half of my brain while working through the chorography of our craft and life. His knowledge and expertise were of particular help with demonstrating techniques for the photographs and for also providing helpful edits to this book. To the list of powerhouse fight directors with whom I have had the privilege of studying and working including J. Allen Suddeth, Daniel Levinson, k. Jenny Jones, Richard Ryan, Dale Girard, J. David Brimmer, David Boushey, Tony Wolf, Jonathan Howell, and Erik Fredricksen (who so graciously wrote the foreword to this book). I am indebted to them for their artistry, knowledge, and support.

I have also been lucky enough to have been influenced by and studied with excellent acting teachers in my life. I must also thank those of my acting teachers who have influenced me the most including James Ellington, Michael Kahn, Ed Gero, and Daniel Kramer. I am indebted to each of them for their rigorous approaches to the study of acting that I have tried to keep omnipresent in the classroom, in the rehearsal room, and in performance.

To my editors Stacey Walker and Meagan White many thanks for their support and patience as I have figured out all of the things that go into writing a book. Their guidance and support have been invaluable.

The visual elements of this book would not have been possible without the skill and attention of a lovely artist, Caitlin Saladin, and the best photographer I could have hoped for, Koko Lanham. Two young actors of great skill and enthusiasm, Teagan Rose and Caleb

Foote, were responsible for demonstrating all of the techniques included in the video links. My thanks to all of them.

Finally, to the brothers and sisters in every stage combat organization over the world, particularly the Society of American Fight Directors, Fight Directors Canada, The British Society for Stage and Screen Combat, The British Academy of Dramatic Combat, The Nordic Stage Fight Society, and the International Order of the Sword and Pen, I am indebted to them for their generosity, skill, and humor through every workshop, every project, and every production where I am lucky enough to work with them. This book is really theirs.

Robert Najarian
Ann Arbor, MI
February 14, 2015

Note

All photographs: Koko Lanham
All drawings and cover design: Caitlin Boyce Saladin

Foreword

*The perfection of an art consists in the employment of a
comprehensive system of laws, commensurate to every
purpose within its scope, but concealed from the eye of the
spectator; and in the production of effects that seem to flow
forth spontaneously, as though uncontrolled by their
influence, and which are equally excellent whether regarded
individually, or in reference to the proposed result.*

John Mason Good

Odd, perhaps, to mention a writing of an early nineteenth century doctor who, in order to supplement diminishing funds, wrote essays on medical and religious topics and, later, philosophy. However, regardless of the inferential subject of this reflection then, it seems in substance more than partially relevant to the topic of Theatrical Combat and its study and contribution to performance and, as equally if not more so, to the training of an actor who may or may not ever participate in a scene of staged violence.

Oscar Wilde once said, "Education is an admirable thing, but it is well to remember from time to time that nothing that is worth knowing can be taught." I would respectfully suggest that many things worth knowing can be obtained by *training* with an educated teacher and focusing on the "comprehensive system of laws" that exist and can be transmitted via a good leader/teacher. This is the proposal of the training text before you.

In the arrangement of this focus as study, and the constantly renewed discoveries of the full yield, stage/theatrical combat can offer a serious actor, believers and practitioners of this craft organized (1977) into The Society of American Fight Directors, a contributive means of continually developing our "comprehensive systems." This occurred only 10 years after the foundation of the British Society in England. Key to that organization in Great Britain was one Patrick Crean, with whom I began my mentorship in 1972, at the Tyrone Guthrie Theatre, continuing a working association for many years afterwards, and whose wisdom we in the SAFD have tried to infuse into all training that occurs under our teaching.

*If an actor doesn't believe he (or she) can do something, they will prove it to
you in the most unfortunate way.*

Patrick Crean

It is – sometimes – joked that since "everyone can act, anyone can teach acting." How many teachers have been heard to say, even today "Just say the words love"; certainly valuable in tasting the words before rehearsal, IF followed by an inquiry as to what effect it is having/could have, on partner. *Why* do you really *need* to speak? Why are you attempting to strike somebody? Generalized "dance" coaching for actors with or without a weapon yields generalized acting with or without staged violence.

Determination of action, based on a particular partnership and awareness of appropriate parameters of respect and safety, denies the need for a director, real or otherwise, to give line readings or a generalized mood to play! It can be superficial at best or dangerous at worst. Thus we, as artists training, as well as teachers leading, must be scrupulously aware of partner, audience, and the technical challenges being transacted, concealed from the spectator, but seeming to *flow forth spontaneously . . . in reference to the proposed result*: predictably, safely, nightly, and effectively for all who witness it.

Mr. Najarian's book successfully argues that of course this can indeed be taught by trained teachers, and the reader can easily deduce the very obvious connection to the essential tenets of actor training, most of which will not yield a staged "fight", BUT, as Earle Geister, a legendary acting coach would often counsel, the active and constant, real-time assessment by each character as to their progress toward that goal.

> *"The question is,"* said Alice, *"whether you can make words mean so many different things." "The question is,"* said Humpty Dumpty, *"which is to be the master – that's all."*

This fine treatise before you strongly suggests that the mastery of self, in service of the art and artist, is achievable and very worth the wide regard it enjoys as a discipline for training an actor in leading universities and academies.

Erik Fredricksen, Professor and Chair Emeritus
University of Michigan, Ann Arbor
Founding member and past President
Society of American Fight Directors

Introduction

Growing up, I wasn't much of an active kid. Sure, I liked to run around the house, shimmy into tiny spaces with my small body, and climb up onto the kitchen counter to reach the cookie jar. But for the most part I would watch cartoons, do my schoolwork, and play video games on my Nintendo (not necessarily in that order). I think it was the stories in each of these areas that I found the most exciting. Stories always interested me. My father and mother were both very good storytellers in their own ways. My father was an English professor. He had a good way of using unusual turns-of-phrase to keep even a pedestrian story interesting. My mother, on the other hand, was Italian and as such had a proclivity towards fits of enthusiasm with her voice and gestures that made whatever story she was saying the center of everyone's attention whether they wanted to listen or not. For my parents stories were everywhere. The act of remembering the stories that they told and the way in which they told them is still one of my greatest pleasures.

Being an only child performing for and seeking the approval of my parents was natural. It was de rigueur that I entertain not only them but also any company that happened to be invited over at any given time. Telling these small stories to people who were willing to listen and watch was always something I never shied away from. Performing ended up being my activity. Before I knew it I was in school plays and studying Shakespeare (and liking it!).

As luck would have it my interest in martial arts came about because of my involvement in theatre as well. Most of the theatre companies I first started acting with would mostly meet for rehearsals during the evening since most of the senior company members had "real" (read: paying) jobs during the daytime. Being still relatively young and with more free time and perhaps a little less care about my financial health I needed a way to occupy myself during the day. That's when I started taking martial arts classes. They were an active, cost-effective, and fun way to keep fit and sane during the day before having to head to the theater in the evening. What I did not know at the time was how much my training in martial arts was affecting my performing life. I ended up improving my bodily stamina, strength, and flexibility to meet the demands of the physical shows I was working on. In addition, the discipline and concentration required in my martial arts training also helped me respond to my fellow actors in performance in ways I had not noticed before. For a while I thought these connections were purely coincidental and had no real practical application to the theatre. That is until I took my first class in stage combat in graduate school a few years later. Almost instantly the world of performance grew exponentially. So and many more connections seemed possible and they were possible through *action*. Even speaking the lines of my characters intensified because I was seeing speaking as what it is, an action. Just like another limb of the body, the voice is a tool for the body to engage in any action that can slash, caress, pierce, flick, tap, or smash another human being to create any quality of relationship.

What you are about to read is my particular synthesis of what I have learned up until this point about stage combat. What is contained herein I have synthesized from years of training, performing, instructing, and gathering information from master practitioners, instructors, and colleagues over the last 10 years. The actual provenance of any given piece of information to follow may have actually occurred elsewhere than the source cited. I have done my best to name the sources of where I had first heard a phrase, been shown a game, or learned a concept as much as my memory has allowed. In fact the technical material related in these pages is not truly original. It has been borrowed from a long tradition of study pertaining specifically to the practice of stage combat without weapons.

There are certainly books on stage combat already in print where you can find similar if not identical techniques. Whether a book chooses to talk about "stage combat" or "theatrical combat" or "violence design" or "fight choreography" or "fight direction," they all involve the same pursuit. This book deals with those moments in performance be it a play or a film where the story cannot progress without a moment of violence between the characters. As a result the relationships between the characters involved alter permanently; nothing is the same. These are some of the most important moments in theatre and film.

Most of the treatises I have read on this subject have tended to focus heavily either on relating technique or anecdotal stories illustrative of the practical application of these techniques. This is understandable since without the physical form of the violence the performers would just talk about it like the Greeks did rather than showing it to a viewing audience. What I have attempted to do with this book is include not only what I consider to be the most necessary techniques for any performer to know for a professional life as an actor (that being said, I am sure the list will be forever incomplete!) but also as thorough a consideration as is possible for the concepts that bind them to the craft of acting and making theatre. I have attempted to combine the historical, the conceptual, the technical, and the anecdotal aspects of my experience and knowledge as evenly as possible. While the concepts of performing stage violence should be omnipresent in performance and in the rehearsal room they really start in the studio. Actors must train the technical form with these concepts in mind or else violent actions will never completely fuse with the characters nor the story in performance.

It is impossible to learn any physical art including stage combat from a book. The text, pictures, and web videos can only go so far in demonstrating the form of the art. Ultimately there is no substitute for being in the room with an experienced instructor to lead the learning process. This book can, however, provide the groundwork and help support sustained study in the theatrical combative arts.

This book is presented in four sections. Part I gives a brief overview of the western tradition of violence in performance and how it connects to human combative behavior. It is my hope that these sections (however perfunctory they may be as these chapters could and should be a whole book unto themselves) can frame for the reader the importance of increasing understanding of how actors perform and present stage violence. Part II provides a deeper look at the particular concepts that should always be considered when approaching any moment of violence in performance from seeking safety to audience relationship. Part III is an aid for training an actor to help develop the specific physical skill set to perform violence. The extensive warm-up, partnered conditioning, and games are an integral part in preparing the movement, reflexes, and conceptual themes necessary for the techniques to come. Finally, Part IV details how the information in these previous sections can be distilled into some of the most widely used and necessary techniques for every professional actor to have in his or her repertoire.

A word on style – I have endeavored to balance the gender representation in this book by including the pronouns "him or her" in equal measure and together whenever appropriate. Additionally, when speaking of techniques I have adopted the terms "operator" for the person initiating the violent act and "receiver" for the person responding to that violent act. I first heard these terms applied to stage combat by Daniel Levinson of Rapier Wit in Toronto. I have always considered it a marvelous way to accurately describe a violent interaction between two people without succumbing to the somewhat loaded terms of "attacker" and "victim." This is of particular use when describing violent interactions where both participants are mutually desirous of the violence that is occurring.

Whenever stage combat is mentioned in print or discussion invariably someone utters a sentiment that has been passed down for decades extolling the controlling idea that stage combat is always safe. Nothing could be farther from the truth. If you are working with a group of performers who really want to make an audience think deeply about the repercussions of violence then there will be nothing "safe" about the endeavor. You will be pushing, grabbing, throwing fists, and kicking at each other in real time oftentimes merely inches away from each other's faces, sometimes actually making bodily contact. Engaging in stage combat requires *risk*. That risk is always calculated and can be minimized but the risk involved will never completely disappear. The only way to minimize risk is to train. Train mindfully and with precision as often as you can. Train like your life depends on it. One day it very well may. Train like the integrity of your art depends on it. Because it does.

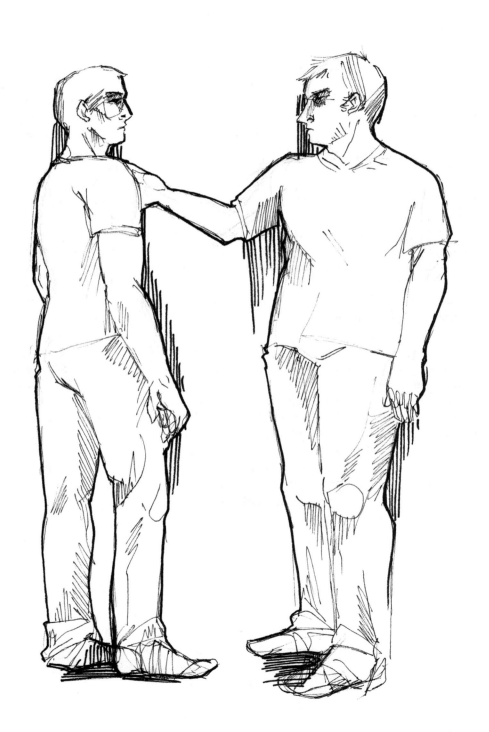

PART I

A BRIEF HISTORY OF VIOLENCE IN PERFORMANCE

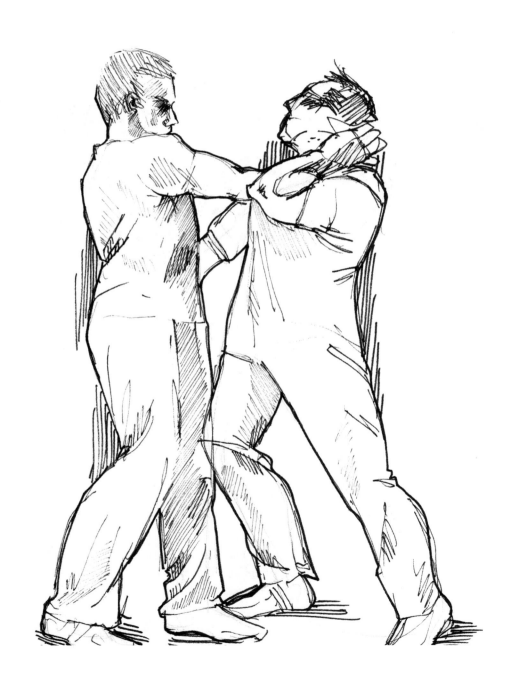

CHAPTER 1

Overview of Stage Combat History

Attempting to assemble much less find resources for a written history of stage combat or violence in performance is a difficult task. Locating books on the subject is not impossible but can pose some problems as those volumes are few and far between in the publishing. The reason for this is two-fold. First, the study of violence for the stage, its concepts, techniques, and tricks is such a niche part of the greater study of Theatre as a whole that the demand for such books is usually on the smaller side. Second, since the need to actually perform these techniques is primarily a physical skill there is little substitute for being in the same room with the person teaching or choreographing the moves and those performing them. As such the tradition of learning stage combat closely followed both its martial and theatrical roots. Information about the skills and techniques used by master instructors and performers was largely handed down orally through an in-person, teacher/student interaction either within a theatre company or a certain school of martial arts. On the rare occasion some written record of a system or methodology would be written down but typically this would be a document that was for internal use only. These techniques and methodologies were often considered to be trade secrets. The popularity and economic longevity of a theater or a school would depend on the ability for theatre companies and martial arts instructors to attract and retain audiences or students based on the efficacy and unique nature of what they had to offer.

If we were to start with the advent of Western Drama we would have to take a look at the Classical World and the roots of western performance and drama with the Greeks. The written material that endures from that time in both dramatic and historical literature bears out a similar narrative. The dramatic tales from the histories of Herodotus and Thucydides chronicle the bloody episodes between city-states, nations, and even families in ancient Greece. With violence being seemingly commonplace in the Classical World one may think that there would be plenty of work for a fight director in those days especially considering most male citizens then were also warriors for their respective city-states.

However, one pass at only a few plays from that time quickly demonstrates exactly the opposite. With some notable exceptions, the act of violence is never shown to the audience. Rather, violent acts occur off-stage, are out of sight of the audience and typically reported by characters through narrative after the fact. The hanging of Jocasta and the blinding of Oedipus by his own hand are told by Creon upon his return. The cries of Agamemnon are projected on-stage as he is murdered by his wife Clytemnestra and her lover Aegisthus and are heard by the chorus who frantically consider what is to be done. The death of Hippolytus, son of Theseus, by a sea monster sent by Poseidon is recounted in gloriously poetic detail mere moments after his death. In only a few instances act of violent suffering or death take place for the audience to witness. One such moment that Sophocles has in view of the audience is the suicide of Ajax after he is shamed by his madness and impales himself on his own sword. Another appears in Aeschylus' *Prometheus Bound* where the titular character is shown to be lashed to the rock where his liver is eaten daily by an eagle only to be regenerated again at night because of his immortality.

These latter two examples are exceptions, however, which prove the rule that the origins of Western drama did not overly concern itself with realistic representations of physical violence on stage. There are many theories as to why this may have been the case, both cultural and practical. It may have been a religious observance that even the mimicry of violence and death in a venue witnessed by others was the provenance of a religious ceremony only and forbidden in any other instance. Also, if we are to believe the stories of Hesiod, Herodotus, and Thucydides, the lives of the ancients were fraught with the constant threat of war, personal peril on an almost daily basis, and the harshness of their environment. As such, it may have been a practice to not depict such physical suffering on stage because the members of the audience were so bombarded by it in their lives. The theatre provided the catharsis on an emotional level without the shock of having to witness actual pain and suffering because it was so omnipresent in the world. Or it could have simply been a matter of practical means, or lack thereof. Perhaps the limits of stagecraft in the Classical World were not enough to support the actual mimicking of death believably enough in front of an audience. Since the Greeks seemed so concerned with the emotional effect of dramatic work perhaps they knew that any attempt to represent death or violence on stage would invariably come up short, thereby breaking the spell cast by the players over the audience and reducing the impact of the catharsis. It would seem that the act of catharsis so central to the art of performance was to be achieved primarily through the act of speaking, storytelling, and the shared word.

This final supposition is of particular interest since one of the main reasons why violence can be so unsatisfying in a dramatic setting is because the physical properties to execute such a grand trick are usually not ideal. We might intellectualize the reason and say the seminal practice of the Greeks of separating what could be represented or mimicked on stage through *memesis* and what could be used as part of the narrative through *diegesis* had far-reaching effects throughout the practice of Western theatre into the contemporary plays of today. Often one will hear the sentiment that the horror that is unseen is more disturbing in the mind than it ever could be in actuality. As Albert Henrichs says in his article "Drama and Dromena: Bloodshed, Violence, and Sacrificial Metaphor in Euripides" about Greek tragedy:

> the most extreme forms of tragic violence are presented as off-stage events, out of sight but very much within the emotional reach of the audience . . . this prohibition of on-stage bloodshed, which reflects the impracticability of its re-enactment, had far-reaching consequences for the representation of violence in tragedy.
>
> (*Harvard Studies in Classical Philology* Vol. 100 (2000), 173–188)

This argument, while having its merits from an intellectual standpoint, is a bit of a cop-out when it comes to actually producing a play. The reason we put on plays is to give form to the formless. The play as written tells the story. The play as performed lives it. In addition, any individual whether a theater-goer or not can likely think of a moment in time where the act of witnessing an instance of violence was so horrible, so theretofore unimaginable, that the observer was forever changed after the fact.

More often than not the issue of whether or not to include a violent moment in a show is a matter of budget and funds since it is hard for an administrator to reconcile spending a high percentage of a show's budget simply on making it believable that people die. It then becomes a vicious cycle for the artist where there is no material support for practicing this part of the art, there is less time given to it in rehearsal, the artist does not get to practice it as much as he or she would like, and it becomes a lackluster skill. The cycle continues when theaters see that the artists have a lackluster skill in this particular area so then production companies are less inclined to encourage it. What happens in the end is that every moment of violence becomes a place-holder, a moment in the show where the director and actors cringe and sigh and grit their teeth to get through it so they can get back to telling the story of the rest of the play. The work becomes under-tempo and out of phase with the rest of the storytelling. Sometimes people try to approach the violence as a problem that needs to be solved only through stylization. This may work if the rest of the show is likewise stylized from a strong point of view. But the stylization of the violence will only be resonant if it is performed in a consistent style with the rest of the production. Anything else that is not carefully considered, well-rehearsed, skillfully performed, and conceptually integrated will seem disjointed and out of place. This is the burden of enacting violence on stage. The obstacles are great. But like any endeavor with a great obstacle, the rewards after overcoming such an obstacle can be considerable. It needs the desire, attitude, approach, training, and time to make it work.

The first real time we see a group of dedicated theatre artists pay particular attention to the role of violence in a dramatic setting is with the Elizabethans, particularly William Shakespeare. There exists documented, albeit disjointed history dating back to written accounts of English Masters of Defence (fencing masters) who used to share the same space with acting companies in London in the sixteenth century. The most notable use of space by the

English Masters of Defence was at the Blackfriars Theatre in London where many of Shakespeare's plays were originally performed. Furthermore, the famous Elizabethan actor and clown, Richard Tarlton, who was a company member of Shakespeare's The Chamberlain's Men became a fencing master (Paul Menzer (2006) *Inside Shakespeare, Essays on the Blackfriars Stage*, Susquehanna University Press). Having an actor of such skill and popularity as Tarlton as part of the company would have been a great boon to a playwright like Shakespeare. If Shakespeare could write a comedic scene that required the deft skills of an actor who was an accomplished dancer, musician, prankster, and fencer he could include such a scene in the play with the confidence that Tarlton would do it justice. And perhaps if he could not play a particular part requiring these talents, then surely he had the skills to teach any actor taking on the part the necessary moves required to play the role.

The model of Richard Tarlton as the company member of many physical skills is an apt one for tracking the careers of many actors and fight directors who still practice and help others practice this part of the craft today. Many fight directors begin their path as performers, typically being taught a fight in a production where they were cast or learning theatrical combatives through a conservatory-style training program for young actors. Interest and aptitude usually prepare an individual for further training and work as an arranger, choreographer, coordinator, and designer of physical violence.

Of course, no skill can be developed and improved without a demand for that skill. In Elizabethan and Jacobean England there seemed to be demand for such skills because the playwrights and theater companies of the time produced work that included conflict through physical violence as a primary means of developing a story and giving the audience something exciting to expect in performance. The physical spectacle as well as the threat of violence became an important device to create expectation and hold the attention of the audience throughout the play.

The use of violence during the Elizabethan and Jacobean time seemed to revolve primarily around the use of bladed weapons, particularly swordplay involving the rapier, dagger, long-sword or a combination of weapons that Tarlton and company as well as their audience would have been familiar with if not in use than in recognizing as commonplace tools for personal protection. Most theater companies would have actors versed in what were known as the "standard combats." These were set pieces of choreography that could be inputted into just about any production where a fight was necessary for the purposes of the story. Sometimes these set pieces would even be used in performance when no fight was needed but rather for when the audience needed to be injected with some enthusiasm. The standard combats were considered a theatrical element to provide just such excitement to win back the wandering attention of an audience.

With the emergence of the cinema as a burgeoning industry in the United States in the early twentieth century there was a renewed interest in using swordplay to increase the appeal of the films being produced. The surge of interest came in the 1920s with the movies of Douglas Fairbanks who was the first director to employ a fencing master to assist a production of a fencing scene in cinema (http://en.wikipedia.org/wiki/Stage_combat). Fencing had been popular for some time and was practiced by many in the United States and abroad as a means of exercise as well as a sport. Swordplay in film continued to be a popular device throughout the 30s and 40s as well, particularly with genre-defining films like *The Prisoner of Zenda* with Douglas Fairbanks, Jr., *The Mark of Zorro* with Tyrone Power, and the host of swash-buckling movies that featured either the magnetic Errol Flynn or the sometimes dastardly but always debonair Basil Rathbone. Any fisticuffs seen in these early films were usually limited to a single punch, slap, or some struggling over a weapon or object. The limits of this were predicated on the fact that there were really no experts in a system of hand-to-hand combat who were available to consult on such films. A few decades later, however, there would be a shift in the presence of skilled martial artists who were available to create such work.

After the Second World War, the displacement of many families from the East resulted in an influx of Asian immigrants to the West. With this influx came individuals looking to find work and start new businesses particularly on the West Coast of the United States where most immigrants would typically first land upon arrival. In addition to various professional skills, many of these families brought over their cultural and familial traditions that often included a lineage of passing down certain martial arts. Also US soldiers who had been stationed in Asia during the Second World War and had been exposed to martial systems in Japan, Okinawa, and the Philippines had also returned home with a new perspective on physical combat as art. These veterans were eager to connect with those people who had immigrated to the US to con-tinue studying what they had seen in the East. This combination of location, skill, and interest that was now present and so close to the film industry created conditions where US culture could explore a fascination with new forms of violence and conflict.

Recognizing that there was money to be made in this new fascination with exotic forms of violence among the public, movies of the late 60s and early 70s began to feature unarmed martial arts more prominently in films. This interest was particularly bolstered by the popularity of the films of Bruce Lee. The success of these films also led to a resurgence of films that featured swordplay such as *The Three Musketeers*, *The Duellists*, and even the original *Star Wars*. However, now there was a difference in the swordplay featured in the films of the 70s as opposed to those seen in the 40s. There had grown a grittier, more visceral quality to the fights. These fights featured more wrestling and fisticuffs in conjunction with the swordplay than ever before. This hybridization of unarmed fighting with classic swordplay with its roots in fencing stemmed from three factors. First, the success of the martial arts films at the time made it desirous for the productions to include unarmed violence, which at this point had become a bit more recognizable to audiences as opposed to the swordplay that seemed more of a period style unconnected with a modern audience. Second, among the artists who started to make their living staging sword fights for productions (particularly for the stage and who subsequently were hired for film work like the renowned British fight director William Hobbs) there was a movement away from the choreographic aesthetic of the classic, swashbuckling style of swordplay movements towards a style that more closely reflected the real-world fighting techniques that were taught by Masters of Defence, recorded in manuals, and used by practitioners of the fighting arts from the Middle Ages and the Renaissance. Finally, a new crop of actors who were becoming popular in the business also favored this gravitation towards a new realism in the depiction of violence on stage and screen. Actors such as Harvey Keitel, Oliver Reed, and Robert DeNiro were blending a deep psychological realism with visceral physicality that needed to be supported by the violent movements in their performances. This new approach to treating all violence, whether with weapons or without, as integral to developing story and character started to take root in the artistry of creating these moments in performance.

The trend in having violence be a major component of performance in stage as well as film continues today. Contemporary playwrights such as Sam Shepard, Martin McDonagh, and Qui Nguyen utilize violence through physical conflict as a main vehicle for storytelling. Audiences have become more aware of this growing aspect to storytelling along with the stage and camera tricks to make violent interactions seem more "real." Now more than ever a careful and informed approach to depicting and performing violence is needed for both stage and film.

There are no new, untried approaches to depicting physical conflict and violence in theatrical settings that necessarily need to be developed. The classic techniques and training to be learned from the tradition of stage combat can be as effective as ever to help create the magic of theatre and film. All it takes is discipline, precision, and consistency. Solid technique, however, is not enough. All of the technical expertise in the world isn't worth a fig if it doesn't illuminate the human experience. Understanding the reasons behind conflict and imagining how a character responds to that specific conflict should always come first. Performers who are then interested in making this aspect of the work a part of their art on a consistent basis must be committed to more than just training the physical techniques. They must also apprehend the concepts of presenting violent action in performance to a viewing audience. We must always first turn our attention to how we cultivate an appreciation and understanding of the principles of acting violence and the causes of human conflict on which the basis of this work primarily relies.

Overview of Hoplology

When there is only a choice between cowardice and violence, I would choose violence.

Ghandi

Why do human beings fight? Why engage in violence that alters the circumstance of others against their will and in a way that injures them bodily, psychologically, or otherwise? Violence never begins with the first punch thrown or the first bullet shot. The roots of violence are deep and sprout into various offshoots of violent acts over a long timeline. If we could witness the genesis of a moment where a strong feeling took root and eventually burst forth into violence we would most likely have to travel back quite some time to see it. The precise reasons for violence are too numerous to count. The catalogue alone could take up an entire library itself never mind the analysis of those reasons. But if we were to work inductively from the specifics we see in the world about violence we might be able to come up with a handful of overarching motivators that lead to most if not all types of observable violence.

- *Survival*. The most primitive and inarguable reason for the use of violence. Even a legal court may forgive someone for transgressing against the law if that person believed his or her life were in jeopardy.

- *Natural / Limited Resources*. You have something I want. There isn't enough of it and I take it from you or keep you from getting some or any of it. These resources can be water, land, oil, food, money, or any other tangible thing that can be claimed. Some of these resources can be linked to Survival but are strong motivators in their own right nonetheless.

- *Ideals (individual)*. A personal code or ethos by which a person chooses to live his or her life. These rules may be so vital to a person's identity that any outside force that threatens the integrity of those rules may spur that person to defend his or her ideals through violent action.

- *Ideals (group)*. Violence can be brought to bear by an individual because of that individual's association with a group. The need for social acceptance can be so great that an individual may enact or respond with violence when the integrity of the group to which he or she belongs is threatened.

These ideals could stem from anywhere: ethnicity, culture, family, religion, philosophy politics, professional affiliation, etc. If there were a membrane that separates individual and group ideals it would be porous with the flow of feelings and ideas between the two. The ideals may not be identical in nature but would more likely than not influence each other.

The study of the evolution and development of human combative behavior is more properly known as *hoplology*. It is the study of the how and the why of people fighting and the cultural forces that influence such interactions. One may certainly argue that the theatre was the original venue for the study of hoplology albeit on a non-scientific scale. The dramatic tradition was founded on stories that feature the existence of conflict between characters. The nature of this conflict may be featured through the psychological, the emotional, the physical, or a combination of the three. Whatever the focus of the drama, how human beings deal with the challenges of existence are given voice and shape in the theatre. Even the word "hoplology" has its roots in a civilization where the dramatic theatrical tradition was woven into the fabric of the culture. "Hoplology" derives from the word "hoplite" after the armoured citizen-soldiers of the Greek city-states who would often fight in employing the main formation of the phalanx or shield-wall. Further breaking down the word "hoplite," we arrive at the Greek word "hoplon," which properly referred to the deeply dished shield made of wood sometimes rimmed with a layer of bronze, although it has grown to also mean any armoured individual. The hoplon was not only a means of protection, it was also a way for soldiers to identify which city-state they fought for. The most reputable fighters from the classical world, the Spartans, were purported to have emblazoned all of their shields with the lambda (λ), which symbolized their region Lacedaemon.

While the exact origin of the term "hoplology" is uncertain, it is most commonly attributed to the explorer and linguist Sir Richard Burton (no known relation to the famous actor but wouldn't that be ideal) in the nineteenth century. The founder of the International Hoplology Society, Major Donn F. Dreager, defined the term in the 1970s as "the study, basis, patterns, relationships, and significances of combative behavior at all levels of social complexity" (http://en.wikipedia.org/wiki/Hoplology). The applications of this area of study to cultural anthropology and military history would seem generally clear. One may wonder if the resurgence or rediscovery of hoplology in the 1970s had anything to do with the cultural shift in the exposure of violence to the public through various media. With the escalation of the Vietnam War in the mid-60s, the US government started to allow more access to television and news reporters most likely in an effort to bolster public support for the war. As a result, the written and photographic accounts of the violence borne through that conflict are still some of the most affecting to this day. Perhaps the most well-known example of such an image was taken during the Tet Offensive when the photographer Eddie Adams unwittingly photographed the execution of a suspected Viet Cong prisoner by the police chief of Saigon.

After a few years of being bombarded with such images the public seemed to become inured to having photographic depictions and written descriptions of violence enter daily life. Perhaps not coincidentally, the film industry started to produce more films where violence was employed as a necessary trope to cinematic storytelling than ever before. An internet search of films of the 1970s quickly reveals the most searched for titles such as *The Godfather*, *A Clockwork Orange*, *Jaws*, *Taxi Driver*, *Star Wars: Episode IV*, *The French Connection*, and *Apocalypse Now*. Also the movies of Bruce Lee such as *Fists of Fury*, *Enter the Dragon*, and *Game of Death* were all released in the early 70s which, not surprisingly, found a new audience hungry for stories that centered on violence and physical conflict.

In the last few decades there has been further development in the use of violence as a primary driver in the entertainment industry. With the proliferation and staggering popularity of video games that have become more involved with creating compelling storytelling, complex characters, and cinematic visuals, there has been high demand from consumers to be similarly immersed in a deep and thrilling experience. As such, audiences have become savvier in the past decade about what they expect when viewing violence. Keep in mind that this is an expectation that has not grown out of personally experienced or first-hand witnessed experiences of violence. Those personal experiences may very well have been more keenly felt by an audience in ancient Greece, the Roman Empire, or Elizabethan England. However, for contemporary audiences, expectations of physical violence have had more opportunities to develop in the human mind out of the images and stories that have been consumed by audiences through various forms of entertainment and media – films, television, video games, sport/competition fighting matches, and the news.

This begs the question, "What does real violence look like?" When it comes to the physical form of violence there is a gulf of knowledge between what *is* real and what *feels* real. The information that the public has devoured is considerable when it comes to the fantasy of violence. Even the reports we get about our soldiers operating in foreign lands are filtered to us through the ink on the page or the lens of a camera. In his no-nonsense and astutely written book *Meditations on Violence* Sgt. Rory Miller (YMAA Publication Center, Boston, MA, 2008) describes the reasons behind this divide. His book is an excellent resource for those interested in the reasons behind violence and the myriad outcomes based on personal decision making in the moment. One particularly useful metaphor addresses the original question, "What does real violence look like?" nicely.

> The unicorn derived from the rhinoceros. Over time and distance and by word of mouth, the reality of the rhinoceros slowly changed into the myth of the unicorn. The process has been so powerful that everyone knows many, many facts about the unicorn. It has the beard of a goat, cloven hooves, and a single horn. It kills elephants by impaling and is strong enough to hurl the elephant over its head, yet it can be tamed and captured

by a virgin. We know all these "facts" about the unicorn, but there is only one true fact to know: *the unicorn is imaginary.*

(p.xii)

Here Miller frames his argument that the original human understanding of violence once rooted in experience changed over time to something sleeker, more attractive, and even romanticized by the traditional rituals passed down in the modern martial arts. This was done through revised personal histories and techniques selected specifically for work in a controlled studio setting. The explosion of interest in the martial arts in the latter part of the twentieth century had a nearly identical effect to how the general public began to view violence through media and entertainment. As a result what a given audience might view as sloppy, confused, and unrealistic may very well be closer to the actual experience of violent confrontation than a fight where the action and effect of every punch and kick are clearly seen almost like snapshots. Film, after all, is a series of moving pictures but pictures nonetheless.

A similar use of visual pictures and images is just as useful in theatrical staging. The process of a theatrical production and a film production are obviously vastly different in their respective execution. Three main differences that are important and central to the division between fights of stage and fights for film are the following:

- *Proximity.* In film the front row of the audience is essentially the same as the back row. Everyone sees the same shot. Especially for fights between main characters, the camera is usually right on top of the action to give the audience a feeling of being inside, or at least ringside, to the fight. As a result, film fights need to seem faster and more detailed because the audience typically feels very close to the action.
- *Angle.* In practically every theatrical space (proscenium, thrust, in the round) the performer must be aware of his or her spatial relationship to the different sections of the audience at all times. Depending on staging someone house right will likely see a completely different view of a scene from house left or in the balcony. In film, however, there is only one perspective that matters – the perspective of the camera. That is the angle from which all the action must read.
- *Sound.* The noise made from fights can come from two places in film: the actors (usually in the form of vocalizations) during filming or by the foley (sound) artist in post-production. Typically the foley artist will insert the sounds of punches, kicks, and other various strikes to heighten the overall sensory quality of the fight. In theatre, the actors must rely on themselves to produce all of the sounds of the fight in a scene.

Given these differences that should be taken into consideration for each scene of violence for stage and film there are actually more similarities than there are differences between stage fights and film fights. The concepts and techniques contained herein can be easily and effectively applied to either medium. This does not mean that every technique is a one-size-fits-all for any given punch, kick, or choke. Every moment of violence is its own entity. No situation of violence can truly be interchanged with another. Each one is particular unto itself because, invariably, at least one element is different. Usually that one changed element makes all the difference when violence happens. Consider a fight between two brothers. They are similar in build, upbringing, and temperament. Despite being brothers (or perhaps because of it) there is bad blood between them and they have decided to settle their differences with a fight. Both brothers are about to fight with only their bare hands in a field in their hometown in the middle of the day. When both are equally matched the fight would be decided largely by strength and determination. Now imagine the same fight at midnight. Perhaps one brother has better sight in the dark than the other? Now imagine the fight in the kitchen of the house they grew up in. How would the confined space change the fight? Perhaps one of the brothers picks up a knife? The nature of the fight has changed yet again. This is the nature of violence – unexpected and sudden with the omnipresent possibility that the nature and mechanism of the violence can change at any moment. Violence demands our attention and we invariably oblige.

PART II

CORNERSTONE CONCEPTS

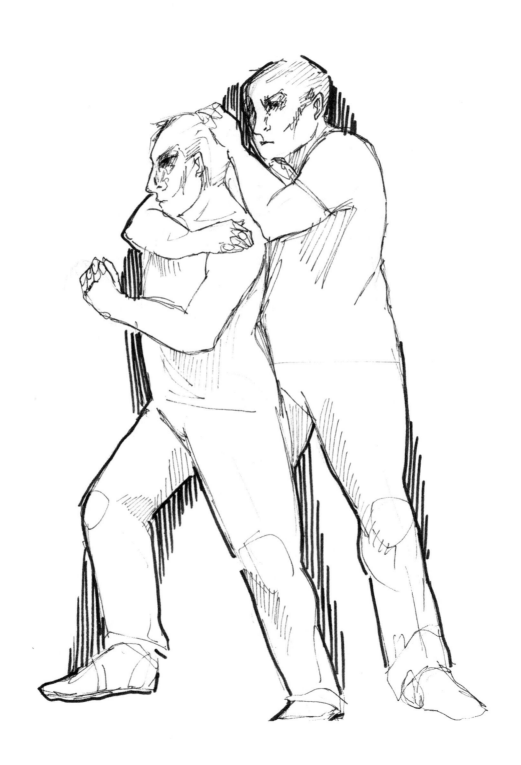

CHAPTER 3

Seeking Safety

Tension is holding on to something that is not there.
Invest in loss.

Cheng, Man-ch'ing

"Can I talk to you for a minute?"

Emily had been waiting outside of my office door and looked visibly unsettled. I had just told her class that they were to choose partners for three scenes of violence to be presented at the end of the semester. To keep things simple I had thought that having the students pick only one partner with whom they could coordinate schedules would be the most efficient way to go about it. Of course, there was a wrinkle I had not anticipated.

"I'm stuck with Tom. I emailed the whole class and everyone already has a partner and no one wants to work with him. I really want to do the best I can on this assignment and I don't feel I can do my best work with him." This, of course, was a legitimate concern in her mind. Everyone has or will be in a situation where something must be accomplished and one gets partnered with a person lacking in skill, desire, or both. Or perhaps the personal social circumstances surrounding the pairing are not ideal. Whatever the case, there are impediments to the work before it even begins because of a perceived inequity.

I reminded Emily that since we were in a training program for actors that this could be considered part of her training. Often in the professional world it happens more often than not that we are stuck with a fellow actor whom for whatever the reasons we find it difficult to work with. This instance, however disappointing, could be viewed as an opportunity to work smarter and with more presence. It could even lead to a better product because of the extra care taken in cultivating the partnership.

After attempting to lead her through the possible silver linings to the partnership Emily fell silent and then drew a long breath. "I just don't feel safe with him." She had played the trump card. This was the one phrase that no one could argue her or for that fact anyone out of. The feeling of not being in a position of complete safety, physical or psychological, is a strong driver to the development and outcome of any scenario especially in an artistic and academic environment. If someone identifies that they feel unsafe it is nearly impossible to refute that perception because everyone's level of comfort with what is perceived as dangerous and what is perceived as safe can be wildly different given the exact same scenario. The feeling of safety is just that – a feeling. And feelings cannot be invalidated. Feelings may be judged (as they all too often are) but as much as we may try we can never negate a feeling in others nor in ourselves.

I didn't attempt to sway her mind about this. Even though I knew Tom to be a gentle person and well-meaning, he certainly had his challenges both physically and conceptually with the material, which could lead to possible safety issues down the road. If these problems had started to emerge, however, I would have been confident that Tom and Emily could work them out with assistance and create a fine final product in performance. But this was a lot of faith that I could see Emily did not possess at this moment. All she could do was fixate on her present feelings. And when we feel our current or future safety is being compromised it is difficult for the mind to focus on anything else.

As a compromise I suggested that the assignment be changed so that everyone had three partners, one for each scene. Emily still had to overcome any challenges of working with Tom but she no longer had to feel saddled by the circumstance of being partners with Tom for all of the assignments. She seemed slightly relieved at this. While I tried to allay any residual fears of still working with Tom the anxiety in her face and body returned even as she was walking out the door. Such is the effect on the human body when we feel helpless about our own personal safety.

This sentiment about safety is not surprising considering the social and political climate of the past 15 years. A premium has been placed on the concept of "safety" in an unprecedented way. The word "safety" itself generally refers to the quality of averting or not causing injury, danger, or loss. As human beings we typically seek safety and avoid loss of any kind. It is a feeling that leads to personal action to avoid such danger. There are more factors contributing to this than anyone could list. It seems we are inundated with occurrences of violent ferocity on a near daily basis, both domestically and internationally. From the contemporary armed conflicts between countries that get so much airtime on the nightly news to the increased awareness of racial, sexual, and domestic violence, it seems that we cannot escape the feeling that we are beset on all sides by a world that is out to get us.

It is not strange, however, that human beings are fascinated by violence. The desire to view violence from a position of safety is very strong. From a distance we can see what happens more clearly, comment on it, and of course in most instances condemn it for being so horrible that it occurred at all. This can be seen even though our athletic contests utilize violence as a means of competition. Whether it's American football, hockey, boxing, or mixed martial arts there is always an audience for spectacles that employ violence as a salient component.

When violence is brought to bear immediately on an individual the responses are quite different and are as varied as snowflakes in winter. Every single person will have a nuanced response to a threat to personal safety that is particular to that person. It's like a thumbprint. No two reactions are quite the same. Perhaps that's part of why human violent interactions are so strangely fascinating. While we may be able to predict what the outcome will be we can never be entirely certain of that prediction. Moreover, there is no way to tell how that violence will be meted out. Quite simply we need to see what happens.

Even though the pathways of the violence are always distinct from one occurrence to another there are three responses to violence that can be applied to every instance whether it is violence applied to individuals, entities, or countries. When faced with a threat to safety the question is simple: how much of this threat can I handle on my own or how much help do I need from someone who is better equipped to handle this threat? Sometimes the mechanism for handling the threat is all of one or the other. Sometimes it is a combination of personal response coupled with outside support. Whatever the particular strategies involved in the response they can all be placed into one of these three groups of response to a given threat.

What I have observed over the years in working with young acting students and professional actors is that for the most part these people fall into the middle camp. When in the studio or the rehearsal room these artists and students will typically defer to an outside source to keep them safe when they feel that safety is threatened. That outside source for a production is typically and should be the stage manager. But in most instances when I am brought in as a fight director to choreograph a physical conflict that outside source invariably becomes myself. In the classroom this circumstance is even more prevalent because as the instructor of record I am tasked with imparting not only information, but also providing a space in which these students can develop a very particular skill set. No matter what the environment there must be a concerted effort by everyone involved to look out for one another so that the task of creating the best possible sustainable performance can be accomplished.

It's day one of a new class for a course I was to teach on American Realism. We were to study the origins of the Group Theatre in the 1930s and work on plays from the American theatrical tradition including Odets and Williams. But before we could jump in I needed to get to know the students. Also, despite being in class with each other for multiple semesters, I reckoned the students could stand to get to know each other a bit better too. If we were studying the origins of the American ensemble we might as well start emulating it in whatever way we could. We started with questions: What's your favorite food? Who are you most like in your family? What makes you laugh? What makes you cry? Finally we arrived at the question, what was your first memory of seeing theatre that made you want to be a part of it. The responses were as varied as you might think from seeing a first Broadway production to seeing an older brother in a high school play. As it came around the group one student, Jake, remarked about seeing a high school production that was enthralling for him. In the act of remembering it he seemed to recall each aspect of the production more vividly as he went on. Suddenly he recalled having the thought, "It's like church, but I care." The words came to him as if by surprise. The class nodded and vocalized in agreement. What was this element of the theatrical experience that Jake had so suddenly remembered? Was it due to the sets? The characters? The story? The music? Some impressive spectacle in the production? It seemed that all of these individual elements were woven together in such a way as to create an environment where audience and cast shared in a common experience. There was, if only for a moment, no division between performer and audience, the stage and the house. The performers and the audience had created a space where for a moment Jake cared about what was going to happen in that space during that time.

When we talk about creating a safe space we need to recognize all of the elements that live in that space and how they interact, or can interact with one another. At the most basic level, this journey of seeking safety must begin with one thing: care. We must care about what happens in that space. The quality of interaction must be attended to and agreed upon. We must first care about what happens to us. We must also and no less importantly care about what happens to everything and everybody that shares the space with us. It is only through examining this dynamic of interlocutors that the participants can arrive at a common agreement of what makes the space safe for everyone.

There is a popular phrase that has been in the stage combat world for as long as I can remember. My first teacher introduced it to us on the first day in graduate school and repeated it often throughout our training. In books on the subject it is likewise stated very clearly and repeated like a mantra. This phrase, by all accounts, seems to be one of the inviolable guidelines of stage combat: "Victim Control." The origin of this concept isn't exactly known but its reasoning seems immediately apparent. The idea of the victim being in control comes from a very well intentioned place. If the aim of violence on stage is to re-create a violent moment between characters that is repeatable night after night, eight shows a week, then it must be a certainty that any of the actors engaging in the violence are not in any actual physical danger that would prevent them from continuing to perform in the show. What better way to ensure this than to put the victim, or the performer receiving the action, in control of the violent situation so that he or she can control the level of interaction? As much as we may rely on others to look out for us, are we not ultimately responsible for our own safety?

With the victim in control, the actor performing the action is essentially along for the ride, responding to the level of violent interaction that the victim is most comfortable with. The theory seems sound, does it not? Let's see what happens when we put this theory into practice immediately. I grab Ted; Ted throws himself to the ground. I push Ted; he reels backward 10 feet. I pull Ted's hair; he thrashes about wildly in an effort to get away. We see the action and the reaction very clearly. Violent action in, violent reaction out. We as actors feel safe because Ted is in control of every interaction. But when the director watches us he or she is dissatisfied. "It doesn't look right," they may say. "What are we doing wrong?" we may ask. We seem to be doing the action and the reaction as prescribed; the victim is in control so we know it's safe, and we're acting the snot out of the moment. "It just seems fake (or stage-y, or wrong, or unconnected)," the director replies. The stage manager has been recording us in rehearsal so we take a look at the video. When we see it Ted and I are a little embarrassed. It does seem a bit overwrought. I'm acting up a storm on the push, showing a lot of puffed up strength but when it comes to actually pushing Ted it's obvious that I'm holding back. Ted is throwing himself violently back upon my hands contacting his torso but the force with which he throws himself seems nowhere close to the force with which I push him. But it's safe because he is in control. What's the problem?

The problem is that Ted and I have had no conversation. Ted and I have investigated the violent moment neither physically nor verbally. I have no idea what level of force Ted can take on the push because I didn't ask him. I assumed he'd be in control so I merely made a push-like gesture and he would presumably take care of the rest. What happens is what some acting teachers would call the worst kind of acting: indicating. I was indicating the action of a push, not really doing it. Ted was indicating the reaction to my push, not really reacting to it. How do we fix this?

The first thing we have to do is talk to one another. That means actors talk to each other, along with the director and fight director and stage manager about the expectations of the fight. First everyone must agree on the nature of the interaction. What are we trying to convey? Do we want the fight to be rough and tumble, scrappy, and messy like most fights between two untrained fighters are? Or perhaps we are looking for something more fluid and lyrical like a fight might be between two martial arts masters. We must talk about style before anything else can occur. If we are not in the right context for the violence the techniques run the risk of looking too neutral, antiseptic, and ultimately unconnected to the world of the play.

Next we should talk about how each character views this fight (refer to the diagram in Chapter 6, Characters in Conflict section for quick decisions about a character's reaction to violence). Do both characters want to fight? Are they accustomed to violence or not? Are other people viewing the violence? How does that affect the way each character behaves while enacting or receiving the violence? These are just a few of the questions both actors should be asking and answering in order to understand the nature of the fight and the characters' reactions to it.

Now that those questions have been posed, both actors can now more fully investigate the form and quality of the moves that could possibly exist in this altercation. If the physical violence starts with a push like the one described previously then there are a variety of ways that push can be performed for both the operator (the person giving the push) and the receiver (the person receiving the push.)

We need to have a common process through which we can investigate the physical moves together. The most common fear I find with actors is not so much that they fear getting hurt but rather that they fear hurting someone else. There are three primary elements to which we must attend in order to be absolutely certain we are taking care of our partners and ourselves.

The first of these indispensable safety elements is *eye contact*. We must be certain that we are looking at the person or object that intends to come swinging, flying, or spinning after us. Now let me be clear – eye contact does not necessarily mean that you look into the eyes of your partner all the time and leave it at that. Initial eye-to-eye contact with your partner can be very stirring dramatically. It also lets you know if and when in fact your partner is ready for action. But once the fists and lamps and chairs start flying we must be able to shift our ocular, bi-focal direction to whatever is most threatening to us at any moment. That means look with *both* eyeballs not just out of your periphery. While use of peripheral vision, or "soft focus," can be useful, reliance on it may get you into more trouble than not because if you are taking in too many smaller, peripheral details at once then you may not be paying attention to the toaster rocketing towards your face.

The partner who is initiating the action should look at the target he or she is attacking. If the performer is attacking a certain body part of the receiver of the violent action, that performer must look at the target that is to be injured. This serves two purposes. First it gives the actor receiving the action a clear indication of where the next attack is coming. In martial arts this is commonly referred to as "telegraphing" a move or to give advance notice of when and where a strike is going to land. While this may be undesirable in an actual fight, on stage it is necessary to establish communication between actors. The more specific the target, the more clear the intent of the attack. When looking at the target to be attacked, the actor should not just think in general terms such as, "I am attacking the leg." Rather the actor should find a more specific location such as, "I am attacking the middle of the hamstring." To go even further the actor must not only know exactly what portion of the body he or she wants to attack, but how the attack is happening (a punch, a kick, a bite, etc,) as well as the desired effect of the attack if it were to succeed (I expect the hamstring to bruise, to bleed, to snap in half, etc.).

Finally, eye contact with a specific target also helps to more clearly express the exact story being told at that moment to an audience. Human beings have an uncanny knack of looking at what other people are looking at first. Looking at something communicates to others that the thing being observed is important. Looking at a specific target with the intent to cause particular harm at an exact moment when two actors are moving in concert with each other is necessary to create a dramatic instant where the audience will actually be concerned about the consequence of that action. If any of the above moments involving eye contact are hazy, undirected, or lacking specificity in any way then the the illusion of danger is dispelled; the violence is lost.

The second safety factor is *distance*. In actual fighting, assuming both participants want to engage in the fight, the combatants are always looking to close distance. Closing distance is the absolute necessary component for ensuring that damage can be done to a human body. For theatrical violence a certain prescribed distance must be maintained between the actors in order to decrease the possible injuries that could arise should the distance collapse. Generally the further away two actors are from each other the less likely an injury will result from a violent action. But this is not always the case. Some techniques such as restraining, choking, or grabbing the hair, necessitate the actors to be close enough to lay hands on each other. The challenge then becomes for the actors to keep a dynamic scene going with changing distances while negotiating a wide variety of violent actions that involve both contact and non-contact techniques.

The third safety factor is *timing*. As mentioned in the training section, use of tempo is very important. We must be able to perform actions at any speed to truly understand them. Let us say for the sake of argument that Ted and I, in conjunction with the director, have decided that when I push Ted it needs to be significant enough to make Ted contact the wall five feet behind him. If Ted is raring to go and moves his own body before I have an opportunity to move into a good position where it seems like I could actually push him, the moment will look fake and unconnected because it is all generated by Ted and not a result of the interaction. If I push Ted before he is ready then it is possible that Ted will be pushed in such a way that he may injure himself because he was unprepared to receive the energy. Ted and I must practice this moment at a slower tempo where we are both responding to each other at every subdivided moment throughout the whole of the movement. Only then can we deeply know what the true nature of the interaction is physically. If we both know the moment physically inside and out then we can make more informed choices about what is happening emotionally and psychologically. At this point our internal choices may lead us to alter the movement in order to bring the physical and the psychological in line with one another. Only then will we increase the speed to see how quickly we can actually perform the moment and keep all of our choices intact. Our top speed will be a *shared speed*. We share the tempo as in a dance to be in time with each other. If our tempo is out-of-synch the pitfalls and potential for injury mentioned above will become clear and the illusion of violence will be shattered.

This is a side note, but no less important – being unprepared to receive force is never a position anyone, performer or otherwise, wants to be in. The body knows how to protect itself and prepares itself to receive the least amount of damage given the incoming force typically by relaxing and trying to match the vector (force and direction) of the blow. If the body is completely relaxed and unprepared to receive a blow sprains, broken bones, or unconsciousness can often occur. It is the blow you never see coming that knocks you out. However, we still need to train the body and refine its response to force as too much tension in the body during impact can actually cause more damage than is avoided. Training to see and feel blows will become important in training to develop the sensitivity to receive this kind of force.

Being able to transfer energy is an important component of being a performer. There must always be conduits of energy passing between performers and from the performers to and from the audience. However, for our purposes here, the transfer of actual physical energy must be attended to with the utmost care. As a result we must now add a fourth factor in maintaining safety. This is the awareness of the magnitude of the *force* being applied in a given action. When either designing violence for a show, performing a violent moment with a fellow actor, or teaching combat for actor training, the most common concern for a performer (myself included) is not so much, "I don't want to get hurt," as "I don't want to hurt the other person." Force and quality of touch must be very carefully attended to so that both performers are comfortable with the energy that is being transferred at each moment of contact. That being said, of course every performer wants to engage physically with any situation, especially a violent one, with as much vigor and connectivity to those heightened emotional states as possible. A maxim to remember is, "Go as hard as you can, or as hard as your partner can take." Inequities in partners during work are common, particularly physical ones. One partner may be able to take more force through a strike than another. How much force an actor can take should never be assumed through appearance alone (a heavily muscled actor may actually bruise quite easily or a diminutive actor may be unusually resilient.) Rather a mutual understanding of the appropriate amount of energy to use should be found through experimentation and investigation of varying levels of force through contact.

In order to methodically investigate the possibilities for contact between partners we can use a scale of force between 1 and 10. On the low side of the scale, 1 would represent a light touch that transfers minimal force. On the high side of the scale, 10 would represent the heaviest hit possible by the operator of the action. When first working with a new partner, it is advisable to only work with the scale from 1–7. When two performers get very comfortable working together the 3 highest ratings of the scale can then be explored. Before each moment of contact, the operator of the action should verbally declare the exact technique, target on the partner, and the amount of force that is intended. For example, "I'm going to punch you in the middle of the stomach at a 6." This verbal communication is key to foster trust and encourage conversation between the performers.

Keep in mind that this number system is not an absolute scale. It is a relative scale depending on the agreement between the two partners working. It is shared between them. One partnership may have contact at a 5 while in another partnership that same seeming level of contact is rated at a 3. The most important thing here is that both partners agree between the two of them exactly what level of force feels right for each number. This can only be done by experimentation, practice, and trial-and-error. After every contact, the performers should verbally check in with each other to make sure that the perceived force of the operator of the action is identical to the perceived force of the receiver of the action. This should be done until the entire number system is covered. At this point the performers can shift up and down the scale at will to see how accurately they can change the force applied in a given moment. Be careful of large changes in value such as 2 to 8 which have a greater chance of becoming imprecise in their execution because of such a large shift in a short amount of time. Once again, gradual practice and communication are vital.

In the examples before, Ted and I establish trust with each other not only through this process of working physically. We also talk to each other about what is working and what is not. But really when it comes down to it no other person, no director, fight director, stage manager, props master, or fellow actor can guarantee without a shadow of a doubt one's own personal safety. Others can help in the quest to be vigilant and participate in helping the actor stay safe. But we have another word for other people looking after a person's safety: security. Security is defined as "freedom from care, anxiety, or doubt; well-founded confidence; something that makes safe, protection." Embedded in the definition of "security" is the word "safe." They are certainly linked. However, it would seem that the definition "something that makes safe" is predicated on the presence of another being or entity. This is the crux of how people get confused between "safety" and "security." As much as the people in charge may talk about the safety of performers through the course of mounting a production, you as a performer must know that at the end of the day no one is going to be more concerned about your health and safety than you (ok, maybe your mom.) Other people can put guidelines and rules in place but those won't help you in the moment when something goes awry. In that moment you must rely on your training and good judgment to keep you safe. You must now and always be an active participant in your own safety. Others can help us feel more secure. Others provide security. Safety is the gift we give ourselves.

ACTIONS AND REACTIONS

"That roundhouse-duck combo was crap." The words jarred in my ears as I sat there and listened to a senior instructor give feedback to two of my graduate students on their fight scene. I thought I had misheard my colleague. Had he meant to describe the students' work in that way? Surely this was some slip or a desire to bring some levity to the somewhat stressful exercise of listening to immediate feedback to artistic work. I glanced at the faces of the two students sitting across the table from my colleague. The comment didn't seem to land on them the way it had been intended. All I could see was bemusement on their faces. "There was no responsiveness to the action of the roundhouse," my colleague continued. "You swung before the other guy had a chance to duck so you ended up missing him by a mile." Of course! The comment made sense after that explanation. He was referring to an acronym used for decades in stage combat training to describe technically the system for not hitting a partner on a planned miss. This has been professionally referred to as the CUE-REACTION-ACTION Principle or C.R.A.P. Most people who have taken a class in theatrical combat with weapons or without have probably been exposed to this acronym at least once. In fact I make sure to introduce the concept and the acronym in my combat classes for the sole purpose that somewhere in an actor's continued training he or she will hear it again from another instructor. I had been in communication with colleagues years ago to see if anyone knew about the exact origin of the use of Cue-Reaction-Action. I got as many ideas about the original use of the phrase as I did responses. Of those, numerous colleagues who had been fight directors for decades attributed its first use to one of their own classes. This phrase has been around for so long and become so indoctrinated in the instruction of violence on stage that its origin has been claimed by the most experienced practitioners in the field. Its exact origins as a result seem ultimately unknowable.

This is not to say that every instructor out there uses C.R.A.P exclusively. There are probably half a dozen other similar sequences in use by instructors. In his book, *Actors On Guard*, SAFD Fight Master Dale Girard uses one such variation. While this book deals exclusively with historical rapier and dagger techniques adapted for stage and screen, the mechanics of initiating and responding to an attack are still essentially the same. Girard suggests a different sequence: ACTION-REACTION-ACTION where the first "Action" is the preparation to attack, the "Reaction" is the acted response to the aggressive initiation, and the final "Action" is the completion of the offensive and defensive movements together, each movement flowing continuously from one into the other. This is a splendid alternative and seems so much closer to what actually occurs between two people locked in physical conflict. If we were to spell out the acronym of it we find A.R.A. It has a nice symmetry to it but alas no linguistic connection to anything other than a constellation or the American Railway Association. Also, the emphasis on the word "Action" is not only put to the fore but repeated, instilling in the performer a sense of the action being the most important element in this moment. Additionally the use of the concept of completion where both performers finish their moves together in the same time is critical when examining the wholeness of the interaction.

Performers are an excitable bunch and as such are typically very enthused to begin at anything. The start holds so much promise. When the moment of action comes they throw themselves into it (Leap and the net will appear!) waiting to see what the effect might be. However, when the moment has happened, they freeze as though they are perhaps hoping to capture the moment like a fly trapped in amber. Then they move on or start again like being hypnotized in a trance as though nothing happened. They do not move through the event, the choice, the technique to discover what the effect of what they just did had on themselves or the world. I find this to be true of many young performers. Sometimes the trap of young performers is to play a mood (happy, sad, angry, etc.) and never waver from that choice of mood for an entire five-minute scene. Oftentimes young performers of talent have wonderful instincts and the ability to make bold choices. However, they abandon the choices after three seconds and move on to something else sometimes entirely unrelated to what happened before. There is no sense of completion of a moment. And since there is no completion of one moment there is no chance of connectivity to any moment thereafter. One must complete a moment to discover the consequence of it. Only then can another choice be made, an informed one, of how one will try to change the course of events.

Of course, none of this mattered in this moment my students got feedback from my colleague. Their bemusement turned to being crestfallen at realizing their work and art were being described repeatedly with the word "crap." I knew they would normally recognize what the acronym meant in the context of an attack that is avoided but in the moment of taking notes on a performance they did not hear that. Nor could they see the capitals of the acronym my colleague was referencing. All they heard was a word that was synonymous with human excrement being used to describe a moment in their scene. As technically accurate as the note may have been the damage it did to the ability of the actors to review their work without judgement was irreparable. I had been taking this acronym for granted for so long I was blind to its implications until that moment. No matter what the instance, I don't want anything that I teach or perform in my art to ever be referred to as "crap." There must be a better way to refer to this part of the work. In scrutinizing the use of the acronym C.R.A.P. I hope to have instructors and choreographers of stage combat re-examine the professional use of certain codified words regarding both the intent and effect of the perceived meaning. I believe this is not only important for instructors to understand but students and performers as well who want to be mindful with the use of professional language.

Let's break down each element that makes up this C.R.A.P. I will skip the word "cue" for a moment but come back to it very shortly. I would rather get to the heart of the matter and the heart of the acronym: the relationship between action and reaction. As it stands with the C.R.A.P the reaction precedes the action. Why is this? Embedded in the principle is the caveat that the person doing the reaction (typically an avoidance of the strike that is incoming) will perform their reaction first so as to vacate the threatened area. The person performing the action or attack only then has the permission to fully realize the action to completion. The sequencing of completing the reaction before the action creates distance and ensures safety. The only problem with this is it's backwards. The physical world that we all share operates by very specific principles of motion. The study of this in its purest form belongs to the realm of Physics. I was not a great student of the sciences in my time at college but I was aware enough (or perhaps foolish enough as indicated by my final undergrad GPA) to take a few courses that covered the basics. Most, if not all, of these courses started with a nod to Sir Isaac Newton. Newton observed that there were three laws of motion that every physical body observed. I would posit that most people would be hard pressed to recite all three verbatim. However, there is one of Newton's laws, the third, which I would wager most people know by heart: "For every action there is an equal and opposite reaction." As far as I know no one has ever refuted this law. And why would anyone? It seems so simple and obvious. If we take a look at the third law closely we see that the order of events seems to flow nicely. The action precedes the reaction. The reaction follows the action. Newton could have easily said, "For every reaction there is an equal and opposite action." What if he had said this? Would everyone have accepted this so well-known law so easily? I'm not so sure. After all the word "reaction" already has the word "action" in it. A reaction is a response to an action. If we were to just focus on the words from an etymological standpoint, it would make sense that the word "action" preceded "reaction" in usage since the latter seems to derive its root from the former. If this is the way that language and the laws of motion have developed the relationship between action and reaction why would we ever treat it as happening in reverse?

This begs the question: how does the person who is doing the reacting stay safe? Doesn't that person need to know what the other person is doing for staged moments of violence? Rehearsal of choreography beforehand certainly helps with this but in the moment shouldn't there be something more to help the performers communicate with one another to ensure safety? Cue the word "cue!" The word "cue" has various meanings. To be clear we are not speaking of the object involved in playing the game of billiards. The American Heritage Second Edition lists the word "cue" with a second definition as "A word or a bit of stage business signaling the beginning of an action. A reminder or prompting as a signal to do something. A hint or suggestion. A perceived signal for action, especially one that produces an operant response." Its initial definition under this heading is inherently theatrical. It defines the word in relation to "a bit of stage business." Since we are speaking of something that has to do with the performing arts then to find this included in the definition should be no surprise. It is also "a signal for action." This too seems appropriate since in this interaction one performer is doing something that spurs the other person to respond.

So the CUE-REACTION-ACTION Principle actually seems to make sense in and of itself. So where's the problem? The problem is that it is completely self-referential. The sequence is simply a statement about itself and what is going on with no relation to story, character, or even the natural world. In a closed system it would be perfect. But theatre (and if I may paint with a broad stroke all of art) and all that it contains is not nor should ever be a closed system. The things we do in it no matter how we describe them must be in relationship to something or someone else. Everything, even the description of technique, must be resonant.

Where does this leave us? Shall we return to Sir Isaac? Let us take the premise that every action has an equal and opposite reaction as true. In this case we will now have the CUE-ACTION-REACTION Principle or C.A.R.P. This, while perhaps initially appealing as another word-like acronym is somewhat unsatisfactory in that the word "carp" means "to find fault with unreasonably." Even though it may feel at times that directors and critics do exactly this when it comes to the performing arts we need not be reminded of it in your process. So let's keep going.

Let's go back to the word "cue" and its innate theatricality. Let's assume that we are not talking about a stylized moment in a performance, not one that requires an absurdist or meta-moment where we deconstruct a physical action and show all the guts of it. Rather we just want to see two people in a violent interaction, have it be revealing of character, fit into the logical progression of the story, and as an audience be moved by it. If this is the case then why have the theatrically technical cue at all? Why not simply perform the action? One might object that this would be unfair and even unsafe to the receiver of the violence in that they won't be prepared for it. But theatre is a cooperative endeavor. So I would assume that the actor initiating the violence would not want to catch the actor receiving it unawares. If this is a well-rehearsed moment (and it should be!) the actors would have already agreed upon when the slap will occur – after this line, before this cross downstage left, when the lights change, etc. So there is in fact already a cue. Why add a demonstrable physical cue when a theatrical one is most likely already in place? Adding cue upon cue only unnecessarily adds to the time leading up to the moment. If we were to do this for every moment then the show would be over 3 hours long and everyone would be late to the pub for the after show pint. And we can't have that can we?

But what about keeping the actor who is receiving the violence as safe as possible? Isn't it worth it to have the extra cue so this is so? If the actor on the receiving end is not actually paying attention to the other actor then no amount of cueing will keep anyone safe. We demand a razor-sharp attention and skill of our performers when it comes to every other aspect of theatre – singing, dancing, speaking, emotional truth – why should we not expect the same when it comes to a moment of violence that is potentially dangerous for the actor?

Instead of having the actor looking for the cue, let's shift the focus to the *action*. That is the important part after all! By focusing more on the action, we know it better. We know where it comes from, what it is in the moment it happens, and what the effect is after the action has occurred. Additionally, by not putting over-emphasis on the cue in the technique, this will help the actor to not over-emphasize the beginning of the physical action. I have observed too often on stage that one character makes a very sudden preparatory gesture for a slap, punch, kick, or grapple only to slow down the action during the actual moment when the violence occurs. The cue is strong but the action is weak. If the actors are truly paying attention to each other and reacting in time to each other cooperatively to keep each other safe then we don't need the cue. We already know when it's coming because we rehearsed it. When it comes down to it, we're actually cueing each other all the time. Not just on stage but in life. We give ourselves away more than we know especially when it comes to where our focus is. So in actuality your partner is already cueing you. You just need to pay more attention to see it.

So we have bid a fond farewell to the "cue." Don't worry, it's still there. It hasn't gone away. We now trust our partners a bit more to share the same timing as us and we shift our focus to the action. Now we have the ACTION-REACTION Principle or A.R.P. One more letter at the front and we may start to suggest that the theatre only comprises those over the age of 50. But theatre takes all comers so let's keep going to avoid any confusion. Let's talk about beginnings and endings. For every story there is a beginning, a middle, and an end. I would suggest that there are many miniature stories for every moment, every gesture, and every action within that story. Likewise these mini-stories, these moments, these actions have a beginning, a middle, and an end as well. The genesis of this story is the *action*. The action launches the relationship and the story on a particular trajectory. Next comes the *reaction*. By reacting in a way that only that character can react to the action, the other actor can have a say in what direction this story and relationship will proceed. This is the middle of the story where the story and relationships can and must change. But does it end there? Of course not because we need an ending! But what is the end to this mini-story of the violent action? After the violence has occurred can things ever be the way they were before? Keep in mind for dramatic purposes there is (and always should be) a reason why the violence was written in where it was by the writer. It signals a tectonic shift in the relationship between two people. Things can never be quite the same way again after one human being has decided to be violent towards another. All too often I have seen good actors who have invested so heavily in a character and a scene throw all that lovely work away after a moment of violence has occurred. Two actors will be so wonderfully connected throughout the scene and then a slap happens, or a punch, or even a shove. And those same actors will play the rest of the scene as though nothing had happened. There is no end to that story. There is no end because they did not take the time to follow through with the effect of the violence and give the full weight to the aftermath of the action and the reaction. There is no sense of completion. We must realize the completion of one moment before we can go on to the next one.

Now we have our beginning, middle, and end. If we put this to our sequence now we have the ACTION-REACTION-COMPLETION Principle or A.R.C.P. The word "principle" seems a bit like a hanger-on. It doesn't really reveal anything additional. It merely reminds us on how important something may be. In my time of studying and working as an actor I have come to realize that most principles of acting typically turn into guidelines. They may start as something we hold on to dearly but as we progress in skill and trust ourselves and the people we work with more and more we tend to rely less on rules and more on each other. If we get rid of the final letter what we are left with is ACTION-REACTION-COMPLETION or A.R.C. Now if we take the periods out we are simply left with ARC. For the word "arc" there are many definitions mostly regarding circles, electric current, and heavenly bodies. There is one definition that comes closest to something related to the theatre and that is the sixth definition from the Merriam-Webster online dictionary: "a continuous progression or line of development." This fits rather nicely into the matrix of anything to do with storytelling. We often speak of the arc of a story when speaking about a play. We also talk about the arc of a character when discussing how that character fits into the story. The word "arc" seems to play nicely with all aspects of our theatrical endeavors.

Changing language, especially codified language whether codified by policy or custom, can be difficult. We exist, we think, we have feelings and thoughts, and then we express those thoughts through language. Pretty soon we find ourselves stuck with a word for a thought. As thoughts change and refine themselves through our experience we find that our needs require new words and new language to better express or define the essence of what we truly mean. The acronym C.R.A.P has done yeoman service for quite some time. As a technical description of the physical process for staged violence it is accurate. However, as we strive to integrate our physical systems with our artistic endeavors more and more, thinking about systemic language that fits in seems to be the path to follow. Referring to the process by which we create violent choreography for performance through the acronym A.R.C is a step in the right direction. As artists we must cease to think of our art as crap and think of our work as having more arc.

Good Partnering: Cooperation vs. Competition

The origins of the word "partner" can be traced to the thirteenth century from a variety of languages including Middle English ("parcener"), Old French ("parconier"), and Latin ("partitionem"). The Middle English word seems to borrow most closely from the Old French word "parconier," meaning "associate, joint owner or heir" (Online Etymology Dictionary). What is of particular interest is the definition involving joint ownership. Partners originally were not simply two individuals who had a shared interest in a common activity. Rather the original use of the word seems to be rooted specifically in the activity of a business enterprise. Businesses are ultimately undertaken for one goal – profit. How one business chooses to define how it is profitable may be vastly different from another. All the same, every business venture seeks to *gain* something. However, there is a package deal to any business venture. In order to truly gain something substantial in business, one must *risk* something. Partners are typically taken on because it mitigates the risk involved for each individual. Granted, partners can also cut into the possible gains achieved by only one individual. However, another aspect of partnership is that two people bring in a certain host of skills that together may achieve more gain than one individual could attain alone with a limited skill set. Therefore the possibility for profit may be augmented by the partnership. Any partnership is a shared endeavor and one that has clear gains and real risks associated with it.

Partnerships, however, have many facets to them and are not judged or described through tangible profits alone. "Good partners" are often described as supportive, appreciative, and attentive in the partnership. "Successful partners" may be ones who simply exceed the expectations of the targeted material gains through the partnership but fail to connect on any supportive, personal level. When speaking of partnership in an artistic endeavor, the focus is often on the quality or art that can be produced by the partnership. However, for performance, the process through which those individuals work in concert with each other try to realize that art can have a significant effect on the final product.

Take a moment and think of the qualities that would be most desirable in a partner. Who would be your ideal partner? No matter what the image in your head of the perfect partner, chances are that partner falls into one of three archetypal categories:

- *The Leader.* This partner consistently leads the action. No matter what the interaction the Leader always seeks to initiate and control the movement or action of the scene. This partner can be seen as in-charge, no-nonsense, and having a sense of purpose. However, there is a trap that this person can eclipse his or her partner in such a way that the only point of view that is apparent is that of the Leader. When two Leaders are present in a partnership there is the likelihood of a stalemate. Both Leaders pursue the preference of their individual methods of completing a task in such a bullish way that progress towards any common goal grinds to a halt. Any spirit of generosity and cooperation evaporates and as a result so does the goal of the partnership.
- *The Follower.* This partner consistently defers to the wishes of the other partner. The Follower never initiates an action or an impulse. The Follower waits for the other partner to follow an impulse or offer a suggestion before responding, usually in an affirmative way that follows the external impulse. This kind of partnering can be deadly in its own way, particularly for actors, when one partner completely acquiesces to the wishes of the other. Here the dynamic becomes such that there is only one point of view in play instead of two. The interaction becomes one-dimensional yet again. When two Followers partner together it becomes quite possibly the most frustrating interaction of all. Nothing gets done. There is no movement and few suggestions from either side, usually stemming from fear that the other partner will dislike or shoot down anything that is offered. Phrases such as, "Whatever you feel like," or "I'm easy," are red flags. If this starts to happen in your partnership, stop talking immediately and just make a move or say whatever comes to mind first. Don't judge it or evaluate it – do it. Only then can the two Followers have something to respond to.
- *The Equal or True Partner.* This partner does not actually belong to a distinct category. Rather the True Partner is the perfect balance of the previous two. The True Partner knows exactly the right time to lead and the right time to follow. This, of course, is easier said than done. To be a True Partner takes the most sensitive and acute skills of perception. A lot of performing artists, particularly musicians, speak of good partners or group members as having good "listening" skills. The "listening" they are referring to is not only with the ears, but also with the eyes, touch, perhaps even smell, taste, and whatever other human senses haven't been acknowledged yet by science. In short, the whole being listens, is perceptive, and picks up on the tiniest alterations and changes in the interaction with a partner, both external and internal, and then responds appropriately and at the perfect time.

Partnering can consist in many capacities and between entities other than individuals. When working on falls I often think of how I am partnering the floor. What way am I approaching it? What is the quality of touch when I meet it? One can partner a piece of furniture. How would you sit in a plush loveseat with someone you are romantically interested in? Or a straight-backed wooden chair in front of a court martial? This is essentially another way to talk about one of the aspects of Viewpoints as expanded by Anne Bogart from the original six by Mary Overlie. This particular aspect of Viewpoints has to do with Space and Architecture and how performers respond to these elements theatrically. Viewpoints is a wonderful approach to actor training, particularly for those who engage in primarily physical ways through performance. Mary Overlie's original teachings are certainly worth studying for any performer or artist. However, for more readily accessible and available texts for the actor on the subject almost any book by Anne Bogart will be revelatory.

In pursuing the craft needed for performance, technical skill is of obvious importance. We can have all the imagination in the world as performers but without the physical skills to realize those ideas the theatre would cease to be. With any moment of violence on stage, good partnering becomes a very important and somewhat ineffable element to the scene. Personally, I most enjoy working with someone who I believe to be equal to or just above my own level of expertise. This allows me to comfortably lead or follow at any given moment without having to be overly concerned about either having to defer to the expertise of a more experienced partner or feeling I have to teach a partner of lesser skill. Additionally, working with someone who is just above my skill level makes me pay more attention. I try to rise to the level of my partner. This not only raises my game but also increases the quality of the shared product in performance. This is, again, an ideal scenario that will seldom happen right off the bat and if it does you should count yourself lucky. In the end, the more you practice with a wide variety of partners, the better your partnering skills will become.

In a short paper co-written by SAFD Fight Master Brian Byrnes and Fight Director Ricki G. Ravitts, the two master instructors outline some fine qualities to assess one's skill and approach to partnering:

A GOOD PARTNER

- *Projects enthusiasm for the work.* The use of the word "enthusiasm" here is a stellar move. The Greek root of the word can be found in "enthousiasmos" or "divine energy, energy from the Gods." If one were to begin any endeavor it should be with this.
- *Shows an appreciation for his or her partner's work.* From a very early age we are conditioned to seek approval from our parents. We never quite shake this desire. So we may as well work with it. Showing appreciation for your partner not only makes both of you feel good but it will invariably enhance confidence in performance.
- *Works to improve upon and expand his or her individual techniques.* A good partner does not rest on his or her laurels. A good partner will always want to improve his or her skill set so he or she can bring more to the table in the partnership.

- *Has an awareness of his or her partner.* This relates directly to the idea of listening and perceiving mentioned previously.
- *Has an awareness of the fight as part of a larger stage picture.* This is an aspect of performer awareness often glossed over. Every inspiring performer I have ever seen possesses this sensibility that again could be called part of the ineffable quality of those actors. Good partners know where they are in space at all times, not only in relation to each other but also in relation to other actors, the rest of the set, the viewing audience, and their function in the story as a whole.

Finally, a lot of artists (well, a lot of human beings) are concerned with being well liked when in a partnership. As a result a lot of people project a demeanor of being nice. This is understandable. The old adage "you can catch more flies with honey" has typically proven to be true more often than not. However, in this instance it is more beneficial to be a good partner than a nice partner. We partner with people in such a way that the interaction is respectful, friendly, easy to communicate, and sensitive to the needs of each other. However, real progress can be made only when both partners encourage and spur each other to do better work. The result is raising the bar for what can be accomplished rather than settling for an interaction that simply gets the job done without any adventurousness. Oblige your partner to respond to your actions. Don't be a nice partner. Be a good partner.

C H A P T E R 5

Audience Relationship (The Third Partner)

> *A play in performance is primarily an object. An object with an organization entirely its own. But it's the audience that works with the author to bring about the transformation. Intentions don't count in the theatre. What counts is what comes out. The audience writes the play as much as the author does.*
>
> Jean-Paul Sartre

> *You can never know what you are doing until you first know what you are doing it to.*
>
> Declan Donnellan

There is often a premium is placed on artistic process, particularly in actor training. However, the most methodical of processes in theatre or film are all for naught if that process does not lead to something that is shared with an audience. Training and rehearsal without performance is akin to a lifetime of reading and gaining knowledge for the sake of the knowledge itself. In the end there is no application to the world. Film and theatre are artistic experiences but they are never solitary. They are by their nature social experiences. It takes a group to produce work in each medium and they are both experienced in a group even if that group is a group of two. Some may put more value on a production that reaches a wider audience. However, for a show to have value the size of the audience makes little difference. The show could be meant for an audience of 3,000 or an audience of three. It all depends on what the artists who are producing the work intend. What matters is that the intent of the performers actually makes a connection with those who are observing. If this connection is not made during the performance it won't matter how many people view the piece; the purpose of the piece will have been lost.

In talking about the importance of partnering we spoke of partnering different elements during performance whether it's a scene partner, the environment, or a prop. Performers also partner the audience. Those who have had experience performing know that this actually happens naturally anyway. It is nearly impossible for a performer not to respond to the energy of an audience during a performance. If the audience is responsive and energetic the performer feels it. If the audience is bored and disinterested the performer feels that too. It does not matter if the performer or the play has an aesthetic of a "fourth wall" where the performers never acknowledge the audience. The performer is always acknowledging the audience and adjusting his or her performance to the energy received from the audience at any given moment.

Directors are always thinking of the audience. Directors are, after all, the initial audience for the performers – the audience of one. All of the suggestions and directions from this audience of one are given with the greater audience in mind. Can I see what's going on? Can I hear what's being said? Can I understand the story? All must be as rigorously applied to the presentation of violence on stage. The best directors strive to know exactly what the interaction is at any given moment as well as how the intent of that moment is perceived by an observer. If a moment is muddy or unclear it interrupts the narrative flow that weaves the spell of the story being told. The moves that make up a piece of violence in performance are essentially physical lines of dialogue. It is a conversation between the participants. If there is an interruption, an ill-placed pause, an unclear gesture, it is the equivalent of someone slurring his or her words or speaking in a strange tone. It will make no sense to anyone.

Directors are a great help in a great many ways, not the least of which is they tell actors where to stand and where to move at certain times. Standing, walking, and talking should be skills that are readily accessible to an actor. However, in a fight with fists flying at heads and bodies moving quickly and aggressively around each other the actor needs a heightened awareness of bodies in space. The actors can practice all they want but in the moment of live performance there will invariably be discrepancies. They must then adjust accordingly to keep the interaction from actually becoming injurious but also fully viable as a believable moment of violence. When this happens the actors for a moment become their own directors. They are self-directing during the violence to make sure that the audience gets the maximal view of what is occurring so they get the full effect of the interaction – reason, action, and consequence.

An awareness of angles is of the utmost importance in performing violence for either stage or film. The angles can be rehearsed and set but in the moment of the fight they can change ever so slightly. Even a slight change to an angle can make a strike either read as a hit or a miss. To allow the audience to get the full effect of a given strike the following elements should be considered:

- *Distance from performer to audience / venue.* The closer the audience is to the violence the closer the performers need to be to one another to make the action seem real. Also, with thrust or in-the-round situations multiple angles need to be covered in the same technique to cover intended targets for strikes. For example, a standard upstage-downstage non-contact slap will never read for everyone in a black box where the audience surrounds the playing space. Rather a V-slap that covers the target for both the profile and frontal views of the performers is needed. Also, the likelihood of contact moves increases with a smaller space. Nothing needs to be hidden when the performers are actually making contact. However, this takes a greater degree of control and physical sensitivity. With larger spaces such as proscenium houses, the performers can rely more on angles to mask non-contact moves from the audience. What this also means is that the physicality needs to be animated even more for large houses and outdoor venues. While the performers may feel like they are being outlandish or like a caricature while performing this way it is the best way to have the action read for the majority of the audience, especially those seated in the balcony.

- *The width of the audience.* A wider perspective of viewers, particularly for a proscenium theatre, or a wide-angle camera shot, requires that the action of any given strike travels for a longer distance between the beginning of the action and the end of the action. For example, a non-contact straight right cross to the head will need to start on the track parallel to the receiver's face farther away than usual. Rather than have a short distance between the start of the motion and the moment when the fist crosses the plane of the face, there needs to be more space so as to cover the target for each audience section. At the end of the action, the motion must continue to travel past the head to a point far beyond where it may have stopped normally. When this is done each section of the audience will read the hit happening at a slightly different time. For a right cross, house right will see the hit land slightly sooner than house left. The aim is to have the action be sudden and committed enough with a loud knap so that the time differential is not too great. Ultimately, think of adding a longer line to the technique. Rather than punching through one target of the head imagine there are three heads, three targets and all of them need to be solidly struck to get the maximum effect for a wide audience perspective.
- *The height of the audience.* This is a tricky one, particularly in houses where the orchestra seating is well below the stage or there is predominantly balcony or stadium seating. The level of the strike will need to be adjusted slightly to accommodate where the majority of the audience is. If they are viewing the action from below, the strike needs to cross the plane of the target at a higher location than normal to read as a full hit. Conversely, the higher the audience is seated from the action, the lower the strike has to be adjusted.

The same principles can be applied when the viewer is an audience of one, such as the camera for film. The best explanation I have ever heard about how to make hits read every time for camera came from a pillar of the stage combat community, David Boushey. Mr. Boushey started both the International Stunt School in Seattle, WA, which trains stunt hopefuls for a career in stunt work for film, as well as the Society of American Fight Directors, the latter of which he co-founded with fellow stage combat master instructor Erick Fredricksen. It was from Mr. Boushey I first heard the term "the golden thread." Later on I heard it referred to as "the silver thread" but a thread nonetheless. This may have been a common term among those working in film for some time but when I first heard the term it was illuminating to me. The essential concept is that between the position of the camera and the target of an attack (the actor's head, for example) there is a golden thread. In order for a hit to fully read on camera the attacking object (a fist, a foot, a club, etc.) must travel from one side of that thread to the other from the perspective of the camera effectively "cutting" the thread. If the thread is cut then the hit registers. If the thread is not cut then the camera reads the action as a miss.

This simple yet powerful concept can be applied to the stage as well. Except this time instead of there only being one golden thread there are as many threads as there are seats in the house. This naturally makes the task of covering the target much more difficult for a performer. By adding an awareness of the elements mentioned above such as depth, width, and height of the audience perspective the task of making hits read every time in a fight on stage can be achieved. But like any art form it takes attention, discipline, and experience to achieve that level of consistency. When that consistency is achieved your new partner, the audience, will begin to trust you more. And as trust is the basis of any successful partnership your relationship with the audience will grow stronger and stronger to the point that they will follow you anywhere you lead them.

CHAPTER 6

Characters in Conflict

Character is defined by action.
Aristotle

Human beings fight for a variety of reasons. Earlier in Chapter 2 ("Overview of Hoplology") we outlined some of the overarching reasons for human conflict. We also mentioned how each interaction of violence is particular unto itself. No two violent interactions are quite the same. It is up to the performers of the violence to recognize the basic facts of the altercation just as any actor would first find out the given circumstances of any scene. These indisputable facts that surround a scene bring to bear how the characters will deal with the conflict between them.

One of the major underlying forces of violence mentioned before was that of natural or limited resources. Let's take one particular example from that list of resources: land. Some people may have had to use violence for survival, some for defending their honor, or perhaps the life or honor of a family member. However, the conflict over land or a particular space is one that anyone can immediately have access to understanding whether on a large or small scale. Conflicts between motorists over parking spaces (I was waiting for that spot you jerk!), siblings over room privacy (Get out of my room!), or live-in lovers who have had a falling out (Get out of here before I call the cops!), all involve an assertion of claiming territory. To begin the process of how performers can organically explore physical conflict we need not go directly to technique. That could in fact obscure the root reasons of why the conflict exists in the first place. How many times have you heard or uttered the phrase, "I've forgotten why we're fighting!" or "I don't remember how this started!" Violence has an uncanny knack of making us fixate on the mechanism of the conflict. It is quite spectacular after all, two human bodies locked in a struggle. The body moves in such strange, unusual, and sometimes (dare I say it) beautifully impressive ways. Conflict, violence, and fighting encapsulate the form and substance of the beauty and terror of which man is so eminently capable.

Despite this (or perhaps because of it) we can never forget the ideas and reasons for the violence we see, enact, and perform. The following game provides a good access point for those who are being either introduced to or reminded of this important aspect of the work.

PUSH AND PULL OR THAT'S MY SPOT!

This is a game I first played in Denver, CO, in a master class taught by Dr. Aaron Anderson, an Associate Professor in the Theatre Department at Virginia Commonwealth University. It is deceptively simple but requires great focus and trust on the part of both players. This game is best played on a clean hardwood floor. If either player has sensitive knees or elbows, pads for the joints are recommended.

Both players decide on an exact spot on the floor. This spot should be fixed on the floor – where wooden boards come together, a certain discernible scuff mark, etc. Once the spot is clearly identified one player sits with his or her hips on the spot. The other player stands about five feet away in any direction. The game can begin at any time. The objective of the game is for one player to occupy the spot for as long as possible. Each player should use only the physical means necessary to stay on the spot or dislodge the other player and assume the spot. Since this is a game, the players are not looking to injure each other. And like a game there are rules such as no twisting of limbs going against joints, striking of any kind, or grabs to the face or neck are permitted. The game should be timed (usually 2–3 minutes is plenty) to see which player can control the spot the longest. Controlling the spot only means that a player's hips are physically on the agreed upon spot. Also, a way to acknowledge that a player is on the spot is to continually say or shout, "I'm winning" over and over again. Dr. Anderson did not include that part of it but I have found it adds an invigorating aspect to the game.

After the game is over and everyone has a chance to catch their breath, recall what kind of physical tactics were used in both maintaining the spot and also trying to assume control of the spot. Usually the players will instinctively find successful controlling techniques to use on the opponent to be successful at claiming the spot. Also, the players should recall the physical sensations that spontaneously occurred when they were locked in a conflict with a clear objective.

Play the game again. Only this time do a slow-motion version of the game. This version is much more difficult to play, usually because when everyone wants to win the speed of the interaction increases. The players should keep the intention to claim the spot clear and present. However, the speed should always remain slow for both players.

While playing this slow version of the game stop every 10–15 seconds, rewind the fight, and see if the players can remember exactly, move-by-move, what they did for those moments. They should treat the moves now as choreography and try to get as close to the original as possible. The players should do this for about a minute, stopping about 4 times to review segments and then rebuild the fight they just figured out in full. Allow time to practice this self-generated choreography until both players are confident in not only remembering the exact moves they figured out together initially but also in restoring the spirit of the first, unscripted game into this new choreography. The game here then becomes how accurately can the partners remember the moves and how quickly can they both get the sequence up to speed while maintaining physical precision and authenticity of intent of asserting dominance over the chosen spot.

In a lot of productions it is often assumed by the director that actors know how to engage with each other physically to fight over one simple thing like a seat, a document, or the remote control. This exercise is a simple, rough-and-ready way to access such conflicts. The main caveats are to build the interaction slowly with intent on the object in contention, be precise in physicality, and take care not to hurt yourself or your partner in the process of playing the interaction. Look ahead to Chapter 14 ("Taken For Granted") for more situations and techniques every actor should have in his or her back pocket for performance.

CHARACTERS IN FIGHTS – SKILL VS. DESIRE

When approaching your investigation of a character who engages in violence, first ask yourself two questions. Does this character want to fight? Depending on the answer many other decisions about that character will follow from that. The character may be looking to settle an old score, rob a person of money, or defend his or her home or loved one. Or the character may be walking home from work and wish to be left alone. The character's attitude towards the impending violence should be the first thing addressed so we can make informed decisions about how the character will respond in the violent situation. Then comes the question about skill. Does this person know how to fight? Is this character trained? What in the text would support an answer of yes or no? The answer to this question is no less important because it will dictate the way in which this character fights.

When I was in high school I rather enjoyed Biology, particularly genetics. Dominant and recessive alleles and their combinations of physical attributes fascinated me. So many possible outcomes from just a few initial elements! There were a few techniques we would do on paper to find all of these possible combinations. Two that I remember distinctly were the Mendel Crosses and the Punnett squares. Both were fine techniques for deriving the possible outcomes of each pairing but I always preferred the Punnett squares because they made a very orderly grid. I was reminded of the squares the first time I was introduced to the basic character questions that must be asked of any character in a fight. Many stage combat instructors have used this combination of questions over the years and divining the origin of them has proven difficult. I can say that the first time I remember hearing about them was through Kyle Rowling of The Sydney Stage Combat School in Sydney, Australia. It is a combination of simple questions that will allow immediate access to intent and deportment of a character in a fight.

We can apply the same Punnett squares or grid to discover what type of characters result when we cross fight attributes. We start with a simple grid involving two traits, one dominant and one recessive for each. Let us call one of these traits "skill." This represents the absolute martial skill level of the character in question. This does not take into account skill level relative to a given opponent, only skill level in terms of a character's ease and proficiency with the violent interaction and weapons in question. The other attribute we will call "desire." This represents the overall will of the character to see the violence in question come to fruition. If we include both of these attributes on the grid in a binary fashion we get the following:

		DESIRE	
		YES	NO
SKILL	YES		
	NO		

Answering these two simple questions will begin the process of discovering how and why your character fights. There are archetypal characters from the theatrical canon who would fit each of these simple classifications. Starting with what recognizable, archetypal character your character most closely resembles will provide faster access into the physical movement and psychology of that character.

These questions can be easily be answered by looking at the given circumstances that apply to your character through the play. Do other characters mention how long and seriously your character has studied a martial art? Is your character the Captain of the Guard? Are you Cyrano de Bergerac? Chances are you are in the "yes" column for skill. Did someone steal something precious to you? Was your best friend murdered? Are you Romeo? You are a good bet for the "yes" column in desire. To discern if your character is a "no" for either of these columns, you must think about the circumstances of the play and the particular demands of the scene where the violence is taking place that would lead the audience to believe that the character is either unskilled or has no desire to fight. Answer these questions for a variety of characters you would like to play and see where they might fall into the grid squares above.

6.1

To represent these differences in character physically in any dramatic confrontation the performer can do some simple body and gestural positions at the beginning of the fight. A body position that has one side of the body in front of the other when facing an opponent may give the sense that the character is wary or possibly protecting something from a threat (Figure 6.1).

That same position with the hands up and palms open may give the impression that the character is being defensive and has no desire to fight (Figure 6.2).

6.2

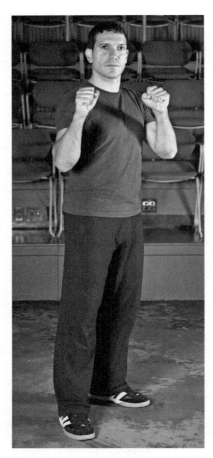

Closing the fists in that same position will most likely give the impression that the character is ready to fight and has some skill in doing so (Figure 6.3).

6.3

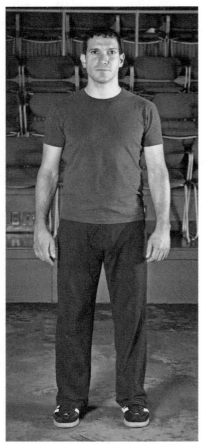

A neutral stance with the feet in parallel may initially demonstrate to an audience that a character is unskilled or not ready to receive an attack (Figure 6.4).

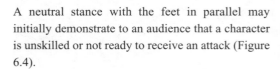

6.4

However, this stance may also be the relaxed stance of a seasoned fighter who is confident in his or her superior skill in a given confrontation. These examples are the stereotypical reaction of a general audience when observing a character about to fight. How that character physically approaches the fight gives a lot of information to a viewing audience about the internal state of the character. These stances are a starting place. However, it is up to the performer to find the particular spirit and intent for each character within the stance.

Of course, this is a rough-and-ready starting place to explore any character in the context of a fight. The exploration should not stop there. There are certainly other nuanced qualities to physical conflict that are extensions of this grid. For example, one character may have skill and want to fight. The other character may not have skill and also want to fight. This does not necessarily mean that the first character will handily beat the second character into submission. Perhaps the first character doesn't want to hurt the second character. As a result the skilled character may still have the desire to fight but do so in a way that causes little to no damage to the unskilled character. Perhaps the unskilled character who may normally be at a disadvantage in this fight has a concealed knife. Any added element to a fight, however seemingly small, can lead to drastic changes in the way the scene is played. It is up to the performers to be thorough and precise in making sure all of the elements to the violence are brought to bear on the interaction.

Keep in mind that just because a character may fall into one category at the beginning of a fight doesn't mean that that character's category cannot change throughout the course of the violent interaction. Some of the most memorable conflicts see a change in one or both characters throughout the course of the fight. Take for instance the character of Macbeth. He is very clearly a skilled fighter; there is a whole monologue devoted to his prowess in battle by the bloody sergeant at the top of the play. By the end of the play after wading through scores of attacking soldiers while defending his castle he is then faced with the knowledge that his adversary Macduff was not born through natural labor. This new piece of information confirms Macbeth's fear that the Weird Sisters had been less than completely truthful with their prophecies and that he is indeed vulnerable. This changes Macbeth's attitude towards the fight so much that he says, "I'll not fight with thee" (V, iii). Even in the heat of battle a character's attitude towards the fight and the opponent can change in a heartbeat. The actor must be sensitive to these shifts within the fight through what is said and what is done.

Try not to make the decision out-of-hand but base it on the clues you get from the text: what your character says, what other characters say about you, even what stage directions are provided by the playwright. Of course, it is possible to simply use imaginary circumstances to create a persona of a skilled fighter or person who is seeking conflict. However, your choices will be much more resonant if they are supported by information that already exists in the text. As a performer it is part of your job to make not only your choices in the role make sense in any given moment but also for those choices in the role to make sense in the greater context of the play.

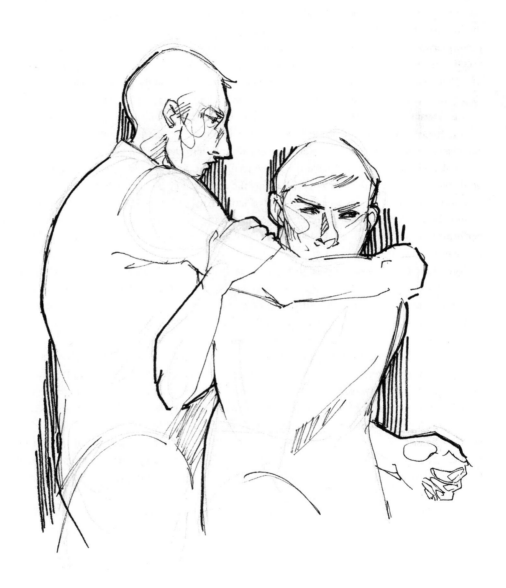

PART III

PHYSICAL TRAINING

C H A P T E R   7

Elements
of Training

Should you desire the great tranquility,
prepare to sweat.

Hakuin

Training to perform violence for use in stage and screen is as useful and applicable a skill for the actor as training in dance, mask, dialects, on-camera work, Chekhov, Williams, or Shakespeare. Studying these aspects of performance will primarily increase an actor's ability to easily perform in shows that require the skills each subject imparts. For the study of stage violence in particular, the works of such contemporary playwrights as Sam Shepard, Martin McDonagh, Philip Ridley, Sara Kane, and Tracey Letts demand a level of physical and psychological awareness of violence that is both explicit and implicit throughout their works. Naturally, one needs not only apply the study of violence and conflict to these playwrights alone. Conflict is the motivating force of all dramatic work. The best drama must involve at least the threat of violence between two or more characters that inevitably culminates in a physical confrontation. The scale might not be as grand or the themes of violence as pervasive as in the above playwrights. But even on a small scale in nearly every story imaginable some form of violence is brought to bear: a woman slaps her lover for insulting her, two brothers throw fists at each other after the revelation of a family secret, a grief-stricken woman needs to be forcibly removed from a home before she injures herself or others.

Despite all of the care and specificity in our acting technique with psychological and emotional truth that brings a character to life, we do the play, the audience, and ourselves a disservice if we do all of that careful interior work only to be sloppy with the form and shape we give that life. The reason we see things in performance is to see the written word made flesh. Having the ability and skill to create highly physical violence that is resonant with the play and believable in the moment of its execution becomes not the cherry on top, but the keystone that helps hold the other building blocks of an arcing structure of the story in place. In any performance of violence it must be appropriate and necessary to the progression of the story, informed regarding the themes and reasons for the violence, and exact in its physical execution.

What does it take to be able to perform violence for theatrical purposes? Below is a list of attributes that should be cultivated in order to effectively perform scenes of violence so that they are *exciting* to watch, *necessary* to the progression of both the story and the characters involved, and most of all *repeatable* for the actors. It should be noted that the word "safety" is left off of this list. This is not an oversight but a conscious omission. The concept of safety is inexorably linked to repeatability for the simple reason that if an actor cannot repeatedly perform a moment of violence without injuring him or herself, the receiver of the action, or any surrounding onlookers then the technique would fail to meet the requirements of repeatability.

ATTRIBUTES OF THE PHYSICAL PERFORMER

1   **Strength**
    Sometimes you have to move a large piece of scenery, sometimes you have to climb up a wall, sometimes you have to lift a body. In performance there will be times when actual force must be applied to an object or body and you will need the necessary strength to perform the action.

2   **Flexibility**
    A flexible body is an expansive body. Flexibility not only allows a performer to stretch to meet the demands of performance, it also allows a performer to fill space by realizing physical movements to their fullest limits.

3   **Endurance**
    Performing shows, especially ones where the physical component is high, demands a lot of sustained energy over hours at a time. If there is a fight, that conflict typically happens during the climax of the story, close to the end. A performer must be able to have sustained energy to keep a performance vital and repeatable throughout the length of a given show or run.

4   **Balance**
    A performer must know where his or her body is in space at all times, the body in relation to the environment, and the body in relation to other performers. Also, making different bodily shapes to help tell a story physically requires putting the body into different physical attitudes that require an acute sense of where and how to shift weight.

5   **Agility**
    Performances are typically snapshots of an overall story or what Stanislavski refers to as a "broken line." Also these stories must cram as much into two hours as is possible. Since

this leaves no time to waste, the performer must have a nimbleness of body and mind that can quickly and gracefully transition from one moment to the next without skipping a beat.

6 Rhythm

Being able to change one's individual speed or tempo particularly in relation to other elements in a production is necessary to create mood, demonstrate relationship, and allows feelings to flow between performers and audience.

7 Physical Composition

There are as many roles out there for as many body types as one can imagine. Not everyone has the same body type nor should every performer look the same. The performer must fit the physical demands of the role he or she is about the play.

8 Physiological Health

The performer must not only fit the role, the performer should *be fit* as well. Please note this does not mean every performer must subscribe to some overwrought idea of what it means to be in shape for a man or a woman. If we were to ask a costumer, being fit means a garment being the right size and shape for the thing to which it is being applied. As such the garment must also be durable and not rip at the slightest movement. As with a garment, the body must be appropriate to a role and last through a performance. The trick then becomes how to develop a body that will be appropriate for as many roles as possible and last through a lifetime of performances.

9 Psychological Health

The demands made on the human body are not only physical but emotional and psychological as well. Good maintenance of the mind is as important as the body to bring both into balance. This is necessary not only on a professional level to help inform and maintain the performance of a character. It is also necessary on a personal level so that the effects of performance are not debilitating after the curtain has come down. Just like you would treat an injury, such as icing a strained muscle, sustained in performance, why would you not treat an internal hurt sustained in performance? If we are doing the kind of acting we all want to do, did we not believe even if only for a moment that we actually felt those emotions on stage? Take the time to be gentle with your mind as well as your body after making such demands on it.

Any training an actor chooses to undergo should be rigorous. The attributes listed above can be innate to the performer. But through the right kind of training each one can be developed and cultivated to exist in harmony within the performer. Often people begin their performing lives excelling in one of these areas. Some are very strong, but lack flexibility. Some are sure of foot, but cannot sustain activity for very long. Some are emotionally well adjusted but lack the proper means to take care of themselves physically. No matter the issue, any and all can be improved. The trick is identifying the blocks so that one can, with help, overcome them.

Training takes time. Depending on the training of the actors, for every ten seconds of violence you should allot at least one hour of rehearsal to initially explore and build the moment. For further refinement, another hour should be reserved for working the moment and getting it up to a believable tempo where the actors can just push the edge of their limits. It should be noted that the edge of their limits is a *shared* limit. The tempo of the fight should be something that is discovered by actors through rehearsal and repetition.

Train the way you want to perform. When under duress, one will default to one's lowest level of training. As much as we may wish it, we will never rise to the occasion without practice.

A NOTE ON ATTIRE

Every movement discipline, system, or style has its own suggestions, sometimes requirements, for what to wear during training. If you were training in a traditional Eastern martial art you might be required to wear a formal uniform such as dogi (gi) for Karate or dobok for Taekwondo. If training in a movement discipline such as ones developed by Lecoq or Grotowski you may be allowed to wear whatever clothes allow for good mobility but must have a neutral color such as black pants and white t-shirts. If practicing Bikram yoga you may simply have a minimum of clothing to accommodate accessing the positions and not overheating in an already sweltering studio. For our purposes, any well-fitting workout clothes will do.

I would recommend a good fitting but not too tight t-shirt and workout pants (yoga pants are great). Well-fitted clothing is preferred as it minimizes the chance of a technique getting obstructed by the folds of the fabric. It is also good to not have the clothing be too tight as some techniques are aided by actually grabbing clothing and we want some give to the fabric so it won't easily tear. I prefer pants to shorts since there can be a lot of falling down, rolling, and ground work involved with rehearsing violent scenes and it's nice to have a bit of protection for the legs, especially the knees.

I very much prefer to work in good-fitting athletic shoes. Dedicated indoor soccer shoes I find are the best for this sort of work. They have decent traction but also allow for pivoting. Some people prefer to work in bare feet especially in the studio. While this is a fine way to develop good connectivity with the floor, I still prefer to have good support and protection for my feet and toes. Besides the extra protection and support, the application of the work in performance will most likely take place in a costume that has shoes as a part of it. If I can get my hands on any part of a costume first it is almost always the shoes. They inform the way a character moves more than any other non-unique costume piece.

Also, take off watches and any jewelry such as rings, necklaces, bracelets, etc. If you have a piece of jewelry that is difficult to remove such as a belly button ring, nose piercing, etc. let your training partners know about it so that you are both aware of it in case it may inhibit a movement or technique.

Finally, if you wish, it may be a good idea to invest in a pair of kneepads or elbow pads. While these final items are not necessary, the pads provide good support and padding for the joints and can be useful especially in longer training sessions involving ground work.

RHYTHM: TEMPO IN TRAINING

Practice does not make perfect.
Perfect practice makes perfect.
                    Vince Lombardi

Static/Non-moving Visualization

This technique engages your brain to create patterns from the information you receive in the body. Mentally rehearsing a drill or choreography can strengthen neural pathways in a complementary way to actual practice. Observation is important! Observation to assist in improving practice relies on prior proficiency in the trained skill set so you can self-evaluate the progress of your practice. In order to truly engage visually with a moment or exercise try to picture not only the visual shape, but also how it would feel to engage with that shape or shapes, and also the outcome you hope to achieve through completion of the moment. Having a feeling attached to the visualization will aid one engaging with the moment that much more fully on not just a physical level, but an emotional and psychological level as well.

Slow Motion Training

Practice slow, learn fast.
Practice fast, learn slow.
Slow is smooth and smooth is fast.
                    Military Sharpshooter mantra

When I ask actors or students to perform a technique or set of techniques as slowly as possible they never do it as slowly as they are capable. The desire to speed a movement up is a strong one. The reason for this is two-fold. The first is physical – most performers don't have the physical control of their center of balance to continuously sustain a move that exists throughout the whole body. The second is mental – performers, especially when learning a new skill or technique or just trying to figure out what exactly they want to do in a moment, have a desire to just "get to it" in an attempt to know what it is as soon as possible. This speeding up is often done without the performer realizing it. Some images to use in reminding oneself to slow down would be to think about performing the action as a Tai Chi exercise, pretending like you're Neo in the Matrix, performing the action as if you were underwater, or for those Max Payne fans out there put the moment in Bullet Time. Allow yourself to be put in a situation where it gives a context to the slow motion. Feeling and seeing yourself perform in slow motion allows for corrections to techniques in real time.

Even Tempo Training

This is the halfway house of training and as such is often overlooked. Typically a performer will perform a technique at a slower pace many times and then suddenly jump to a considerable faster speed. Increasing speed and tempo should always be a gradual progression. After knowing the technique and a physical moment backwards and forwards from slow training, the tempo should be increased gradually *through* medium speed training. At its best, medium speed training should look like a cooperative dance moved through at a smooth, even tempo between both performers.

Full Throttle Training

Eventually the performers will begin to discover where their shared limit of speed exists for the performance. The more the moment is practiced, the more quickly the performers will be able to react to each other. This will develop reaction speed, distancing, and more ease coping with possible psychological stress in a high-speed situation. Moreover this pressure that naturally occurs by training at full speed, or as fast as each performer can manage, will start to reveal gaps in technique. If the technique breaks down or accuracy is sacrificed for speed, that is an indication that the performers have not truly connected with the shared moment involving the technique nor the reason supporting its use. In this case, the performers should begin again in slow motion to trouble shoot where the gaps lie.

If the choreography is simply performed for speed, storytelling and character typically become muddy or lost altogether. The moves must have velocity and direction towards an exact target to carry the audience along with the characters. Remember that true speed is a function of accuracy.

WARMING UP

There was a long time in my life when warming up seemed like a colossal waste of time. I thought that warm-ups were for old men whose bodies had ossified to the extent that in the absence of a warm-up their bodies would break or even turn to dust. Warm-ups only delayed getting to the good stuff; the good stuff being the actual scene work, topics, or activities that I was there to work on, assimilate, and from which I was supposed to benefit.

Every decent director, instructor, or coach in nearly every field, subject, or sport I have participated in over my life start their rehearsals, classes, or practices with a warm-up, however brief. When working with the UK-based immersive theatre group Punchdrunk, every day begins with a one-hour warm-up (which is essentially a master class with different members of the ensemble leading each day) consisting of stretching, dance technique, combinations, and partnering exercises before beginning the day's rehearsal of demanding physical composition. Judy Braha, a stellar teacher and director at Boston University, begins every class or rehearsal with a traditional theatrical group warm-up involving vocal, physical, impulse, and partnering exercises before initiating work for the day. J. Ed Azaria, a core company member from the SITI Company, begins his dramaturgy classes with 5 minutes of free writing or writing about a topic to be discussed during the class. Jae Hun Kim, the world-renowned Taekwondo Grandmaster who teaches in Boston, MA, begins all of his classes with a series of exercises designed to loosen the shoulder girdle, hips, and spine in order for students to execute strikes with more power and precision. These warm-ups do not merely serve as a filler of time until a group of people are finally ready to engage with the activities of the day. Warming up prepares us for what is to come. It gently coaxes the body and the mind to engage with what is being presented, fertilizing the soil so that what is planted there later on may more easily take root.

There was always a question in my mind about whether or not warming up actually prevented me from injuring myself in any physical way during the day's activities. There was a time when I could jump into nearly any activities and, while I may have been a bit sorer the next day if I had not warmed up, I could still complete the physical activities without hurting myself. There have been various studies conducted that support the claim that warming up does seem to help prevent injuries. However, there have been equally if not more numerous studies that have shown that warming up does not significantly decrease the likelihood of injury. If you are young and in perfect physical condition with no previous injuries then it is unlikely that you will injure yourself if you choose to skip a warm-up. I would like to point out that those studies nearly always say that warming up does not *significantly* reduce the likelihood of injury. Without knowing if the use of the word "significant" refers to a statistical significance or a significance with regard to the degree to which a body may become injured would need to be investigated for each study. However, in my mind, if any warming up would afford me the luxury of avoiding any kind of injury later on, significant or non-significant, I would rather take the 5–10 minutes to warm up than deal with even a minor strain later in the day.

As the body ages (and I speak from some personal experience) it takes a bit longer to rev up to activity. Warming up allows for a natural elongation and plasticity of the musculature and pumps more blood to all areas of the body. When training in Taekwondo, I can never kick as high on an axe kick or swing as freely on a spinning backfist right out of the gate as I can after having warmed up my arms and legs with limb swings from the major joints and dynamic stretching. Additionally, collagen in the skin can change forms from solid to a more gel-like liquid depending on the time it is massaged and coaxed and stretched. Taking even a few minutes to warm up allows the collagen in the skin to become less rigid allowing for more supple and fluid movement.

Any time I think of skipping even a perfunctory warm-up before a work session, rehearsal, or performance I just need to remind myself of one aspect of the things mentioned above and I gladly start moving around. It has taken some time to recognize all of this but finally the individual benefits of warming up seem obvious to me. However, the benefits of warming up with others are even more beneficial when helping to foster a group dynamic. Warming up centers us physically and mentally so that we can then extend our energies to connect to others with whom we share space whether on a stage or in a studio. Warming up is time when we initially come together to establish connection with each other through a common endeavor. The sparks of energy that create a dynamic interaction between bodies begin here during the warm-up.

BASIC WARM-UP

Use of Music during Training

I prefer to warm up and train with music. Any genre that you like will be good to spur you to motion and shuffle off the omnipresence of inertia. Oftentimes the musical selection will depend on what kind of mood or aural framework I would like to set for the techniques or style of fight for the day. If we are working on classic American Western fisticuffs, I might put on the soundtrack from the *Magnificent Seven* or *Silverado*. If we are working on controlling moves such as hair grabs, pushes, shirts grabs, and the like I may put on some Big Band music since the contact nature of the moves requires the same kind of kinesthetic partnering as swing dancing. If we are doing a modern martial arts style of fight I may put on the soundtrack to *The Matrix*. Training while different types of music are playing also allows your body to move and respond to different tempos, which is an extremely important ability to develop in this work.

The Sequence

The first few minutes of any warm-up should be spent getting the blood flowing to all of the extremities. Some people go right to static stretching off the bat. While this may feel good in the moment, you will not get as much benefit from stretching a cold muscle as you will a warm one. When starting off a work session, I typically enjoy doing some light jogging followed by basic plyometrics such as high skipping, leaping side steps, and grapevines. These exercises require the body to use proprioception while cultivating important attributes in stage combat such as balance, agility, and coordination. Also, the focus on footwork and the explosive action of the larger muscles in the legs warms the entire body up more quickly than warm-ups that begin with smaller muscle groups.

Everyone should have their favorite sequence for warming up depending on the activity they are about to do. The following series I have found to be time efficient and suitable for preparing to train in stage combat. It helps to free the body of extraneous tension, find grounding through the center during motion, and prepares the spine and joints for a lot of the twisting and turning that is inherent in moving with high kinetic energy and violent intent.

For each of the following movements remember to stay relaxed and perform each exercise for at least 30 seconds. One to two minutes is ideal but in rehearsal there is only so much time to practice. A warm-up is, after all, a useful tool in order to do better work. Devote at least 15% of your time to warming up and 5% to cooling down with 80% of the time devoted to the particular work focus for the session. Above all, stay relaxed during the warm-up. If you are tense from life outside the studio, allow the warm-up to help you relax.

Plant the soles of your feet on the ground and shake various body parts to initiate increased blood flow throughout the body. Start with light to vigorous shaking of the hands followed by light to vigorous shaking of the arms, followed by light to vigorous shaking of the whole body. Each of these should take place for about 15–20 seconds. While moving a specific body part, try to focus on moving the joint above the specific appendage so as to

7.2

7.3

7.4

7.5

minimize the muscular exertion on that specific limb. For example, when shaking the hands, try to only move from the wrist. When shaking the arms out, only move from the shoulders. When shaking the entire body, feel a firm connection through the soles of your feet to the floor and gently bounce in your knees so that your entire body moves up and down. The point here is to minimize the muscular tension we think is necessary for motion and begin to think about economizing movement.

Next, in order to wake up the structures supporting the spine, place your feet about 1½ or 2 times your shoulder width apart and twist at the waist allowing your arms to hang completely free like wet noodles or the velvet ropes outside of that restaurant where you made reservations months ago to get a table. Twist your hips so that the body remains upright and the soles of the feet remain on the ground. Twist clockwise until you reach the limit of motion and then twist counter-clockwise in the same way. Do this 4 to 5 times in each direction. Then increase the torque of your twist and allow the back heel of the left foot to come up off the floor as you twist clockwise. While you are twisting you should feel a grounding feeling through your body as you contact the floor with the sole of the right foot and the ball of the left foot. You should eventually be twisting with enough force that as the hips twist the body, the arms follow and fly up and out like helicopter blades until they settle and make a slapping sound on the body when you reach the limit of motion for your twist. Do this in each direction at least 5 times (Figures 7.2–7.5).

Remember to keep your arms completely free of tension. This will encourage more blood flow to the hands. You may even feel a bit of a warm tingling feeling in your fingers, a good sign that blood is flowing freely. There is a tendency here to rise or arabesque as one twists. Try to engage with a feeling of lowering the center as you twist into the movement. This will not only improve balance, it will also inform a lot of techniques that require demonstrating power and force through use of the entire body.

Don't neglect to try to get a slapping sound on the body when the loose arms and hands contact it at the extremities of the twist. Keeping the arms and hands loose will tend to produce a louder and more resonant sound. This is helpful in our training for two reasons. First, the act of having the body stuck in this manner will prime the skin and get us physically and mentally ready for the contact techniques we will want to practice. And second, getting used to a loose hand making sound on the body will become extremely important when it comes to the technique of knapping, or the sound created by the hand against the other hand or another part of the body to simulate violent contact. Having a loose hand will be effective in making better, more resonant sound when contacting the body. It will also hurt less. We will be asking a lot of our hands so best to get them ready as soon as possible.

Place the feet a bit more than two times shoulder width with the legs straight. Knees should have the slightest bend in them and not be locked. Reach both arms and fingers up to the sky and stretch. Extend the arms and torso up and out and rotate at the waist as though describing a circle with the fingertips round the entire body in a clockwise manner. The bottom half of the body should be stable but the upper half should swing slowly around

7.6

7.7

7.8

7.9

7.10

in a constant motion while reaching and stretching continually 360 degrees. Make certain not to rotate the torso so fast that you get dizzy. After 4 or 5 times in one direction, start to rotate the other way in the same fashion (Figures 7.6–7.9).

Support your body on the right foot while placing the toes of the left foot on the floor (if not wearing shoes then place the ball of left foot firmly on the floor.) Without losing contact with the floor move the ankle in a circular motion 6–8 times, clockwise then counter-clockwise. When done with the left ankle, repeat with the right ankle. When warming up the ankles and moving them in this way, feel that the circular motion is originating in the hip socket rather than the ankle joint. This will allow the musculature around the ankle to be more relaxed and loosen up a bit more easily (Figure 7.10).

While standing, put the feet together, soles flat on the floor. Bend the knees and place the hands above the knees. Move the knees clockwise circularly to explore the range of motion in your knees. Try to keep the soles of the feet as flat on the floor as possible. Explore the limits of your knee flexibility without sacrificing support from your feet underneath. Rocking on to the sides of the feet during this exercise will lead to an unsupported position for the knees and will actually cause stress to the joint (Figures 7.11–7.13).

7.11   7.12   7.13

Keeping the feet together, stand and apply the same circular motion to the hips, clockwise then counter-clockwise 6–8 times each. Try to localize the movement to the hips without moving the upper body, particularly the head, too much. After completing both sides, separate the feet to shoulder width apart. Isolate the pelvis and move it in a circular motion 6–8 times clockwise then counter-clockwise. The aim here is to isolate the pelvic girdle and sacrum portion of the spine without causing too much secondary motion below the knees or above the navel. As with the other joints, try to make as large of a circle as possible without moving other structures of the body. If moving the pelvis in this manner seems odd or difficult then reduce it to movements in 4 directions. If you imagine your pelvis is a big bowl filled with water, start by tipping the bowl in such a way that the water will spill out behind you. This will take the pelvis up and forward elongating the spine and taking the curve out of your back. Now reverse the process and tip the bowl in such a way that the water will spill in front of you. This takes the pelvis down and back increasing the sway in the back. Next, tip the bowl so that the water spills to the right. This takes the pelvis up to the left and should create the feeling that the left leg is slightly longer than the right. Now tip the bowl so that the water is spilling to the left. The pelvis should be up and to the right creating a feeling of elongation in the right leg. Practice moving through those four points of pelvic direction. Once you get comfortable with those you can start moving the pelvis on the diagonal and increase your pelvic motion to eight points. Eventually you should be able to more easily find the fluidity of moving the pelvis and sacrum in an isolated circular motion. (Note: If you continue to find it difficult to feel the motion of the pelvis and sacrum standing up, try the same exercise up against a wall or lying down on the floor. Having a solid object against the hips oftentimes helps to figure out where in space they are and what position they are in.)

Using the same circular motion, center the movement in the middle of the spine corresponding to the middle of the sternum on the front of the body. This will effectually move the thoracic region of the torso or ribcage in a similar way to the pelvis. The difference here is that the motion does not tip the ribcage as we did with the pelvis. Rather the ribcage should move on a level, horizontal plane during this motion. As with the pelvis, the motion here should be smooth and continuous. Likewise, try not to move the head or hips too much during this motion. Try to localize the motion specifically in the thoracic region of the spine and torso. If moving the ribcage in this manner proves difficult, we can follow similar steps outlined above for the pelvis to accentuate the kind of spinal articulation possible with the torso. First jut the chest out and throw the shoulders back as far as possible. This brings not only the chest but also the spine forward in space. Next reverse the motion and make the chest concave by pushing the sternum in and back. This should also bring the shoulders forward. The back should start to round as a result, bringing the spine backwards in space. Next try translating the entire ribcage to the right. This is a simple translation in space. No tipping or turning the ribcage is necessary. Simply try to displace the ribcage a few inches to the right. This will in turn make the spine curve to the right as well. The same thing can be done by moving the ribcage to the left side of the body, thereby giving the spine a curve to the left. Once these four points have been accessed, then try to find points on the diagonals – forward and to the right, forward to the left, back and to the left, and back and to the right. Eventually you should be able to smooth out the transitions between these points to create a wide circular motion. (If you ever have trouble feeling your torso and ribcage moving in the direction you want, place a relaxed hand on the sternum to get extra tactile feedback.)

Move up the spine to the head. A lot of warm-ups do and should include rotating the head and neck. Since this is still a warm-up we must be very careful not to do too much too soon with the muscles surrounding the cervical spine. Performing movement that is too fast, sudden, or exceeds the range of motion before properly warming up the muscles in the neck first can lead to even minor strains that will significantly affect training and performance. The motion of the head should be connected and supported by the shoulder girdle and down the rest of the thoracic spine. There should be movement support from the base structure of the shoulders so that the muscles minimize the chance of overtaxing the neck muscles. Think of making the muscles in the neck very long and continuous from the base of the shoulders up through the connections to the skull and other bones in the head. Now with these long muscles, start to make small circles with the head in a clockwise direction. You can increase the area of the circle gradually up to 8 times in one direction to as large a circumference as is comfortable. Switch the direction of the circle after 8 times to balance the muscles.

Warming the body initially through motion will begin to increase the plasticity of the muscles and connective tissue of the body as well as naturally increase range of motion. Once these structures are more supple, static stretching can now lengthen them further. Now that the more kinetic part of the warm-up has occurred static stretching can be better utilized to further lengthen and release extraneous tension in the muscles. The major locations where the effects of limbering up will most greatly be felt are in the shoulder and hip girdles and the major muscle groups that surround them.

Tilt the head to the right so that the right ear is hovering above the right shoulder. Take care not to over-exert the head or engage the neck muscles for the tilt. Simply let the weight of the head give over to gravity and allow the muscles to loosen. Also, try to resist the urge to have the shoulders rise during this neck release. After a few moments bring the right hand up and over the top of the head so that the right hand is resting gently against the left side of the head. The right hand will most likely be partially covering the left ear. Try not to pull the head down with the right hand. Rather let the added weight of the arm allow the neck muscles to be stretched a bit farther. After a few moments in this position, float the left arm up so that it is parallel with the ground and reach out from the shoulder girdle and back. Make sure to extend from the elbow as well. Now point the fingers to the ceiling as much as possible. Ideally the palm and fingers of the left hand should be completely perpendicular to the left arm. Different people feel the stretch here in different places. Personally I typically feel the most sensation through the side of the neck being stretched, through the bicep, down through the front part of the forearm, and out to the muscles in my thumb, index, and middle fingers. This can be a wonderful release for not only the muscles but also the fasciae in the neck and arms (Figure 7.14).

7.14

Place the arms outstretched from the sides of the body and parallel to the floor with the palms facing up. Make small, tight circles with the arms moving forward towards the front of the body. With each circle make the circumference of the circle progressively larger. When the maximum circumference is reached reverse the direction of the circle. The arms should now be moving in large backward circles. With each subsequent repetition make the circles smaller and smaller until the arms have returned to tight circles once again.

Now, take the right elbow and place it over and past the inside of the left elbow. Then bend the left elbow so that the left hand points straight up to the ceiling making a "plus sign" with both arms. Next bend the right elbow and wrap the right forearm around the left forearm until the right palm and the left palm can meet and press together. This would be essentially a position of prayer for the hands normally, only now the arms are intertwined like vines. In yoga this is commonly referred to as "Eagle Arms." Now settle the shoulders down and play with the elbows moving up and away from the body. This should start to loosen up the deltoids, rotators, and structures surrounding the shoulder. If this position is cumbersome or you are not feeling a stretch in this position, then simply stop at the "plus sign" and hug the right arm in and across the body. Repeat with the left arm on top of the cross of arms to balance out the sides (Figures 7.15–7.16).

7.15

7.16

While in a standing position, balance on the right foot while placing the left ankle over the right quadricep. Bend the right standing leg to as low as it will go while keeping the knee of the bent left leg pointing straight out to the left. This should feel similar to sitting "business-style" in a chair. This position not only works on balance, strength, and stability for the supporting structures of the right ankle but also gives a good stretch to the muscles in the hips such as the gluteals and piriformis.

7.17

Both of the above positions can be combined to further develop balance.

Place the feet together and stand up in a straight and relaxed neutral position. Now interlace the fingers, straighten the arms, and reach them over the head, palms facing up as though pressing the ceiling above. Reach the arms up and back to further loosen the shoulders. Try to resist the sternum rising and as a consequence the lumbar region of the back shortening. Rather keep the spine neutral and long while being supported by the core muscles. Take a deep breath in and on the exhale twist the whole body from the trunk and look to the right. Make certain not to over-rotate here. This position of torsion is a delicate one for the knees, hips, and muscles supporting the spine. Only go as far as the limits of your body allow on any particular day. Take another deep breath in this position and let out a long exhale. Return to neutral, inhale deeply and on the exhale repeat the same torsion looking to the left (Figures 7.18–7.19).

7.18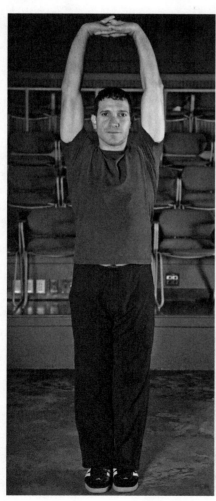

7.19

After returning to neutral, grasp the left wrist with the right hand, inhale deeply and on the exhale bend sideways at the waist reaching the left palm up and over to the right. Rather than thinking of shortening the right side of the body, think of lengthening the left side of the body. Here a stretch should be felt in the latissimus dorsi, the broadest muscle of the back that runs from below the shoulders, behind the arms, and attaches to the lower spine. Take several deep breaths while stretching here thinking about lengthening the left side on each exhale. Return to neutral on an exhale and then repeat on the opposite side (Figure 7.20).

7.20

After stretching both sides of the torso, reach down to stretch the hamstrings and lower back. There are many variations on this position to isolate a deeper stretch, particularly in the hamstrings. Keeping the back straight will isolate more of a stretch in the hamstrings while rounding the spine will stretch more of the musculature of the back (Figure 7.21). One variation that I have found very challenging is while in the folded position, bending the knees, resting the torso on the quadriceps and crossing the arms behind and through the legs so that the right hand is grasping the left shin and the left hand is grasping the right shin (Figure 7.22). On a deep exhalation allow the legs to straighten without losing the grasp on the shins. If this stretch proves challenging in the standing position, try performing it seated on the floor using the same cross of the arms through the legs and grasping the shins. Then extend the legs out in front to achieve a variation of this very deep stretch of the hamstrings.

7.21

7.22

7.23

Keeping the soles of the feet on the floor, bend the knees and squat down. You may find that the heels will automatically come up off the floor. In order to find some flexibility in the ankles, experiment to see how close the feet can be together without the heels coming up off the floor. Start with them wide and then inch them closer and closer until you find the limit. Eventually over time the ankles will loosen more and more to the point where the instep of the feet can be touching and the heels will remain on the floor. If this position is already achievable, try the same position while clasping the hands behind the back for an added challenge (Figure 7.23).

7.24

Still in the squatting position, balance on the balls of the feet while bouncing lightly up and down and from side to side to work out any further spots of extraneous tension in the lower joints (Figure 7.24).

Pop up into a wide dancer's second position with the feet, toes and knees pointed out and to the sides (Figure 7.25). Bend the knees and place the back of the forearms on the inside of the thighs. Lower the hips as though sitting down while pressing out with the forearms, separating the knees farther apart. This stretch isolates the adductor muscle groups on the inside of the thighs (Figure 7.25).

7.25

Slowly extend the legs and walk the feet out farther away from each other and point the toes forward. Bend at the waist moving the hips back and keeping the back straight. Supporting the stretch with the hands on the floor can be useful in keeping balance if necessary. Walk the hands over to the right foot and pull the torso as close to the leg as possible. Walk the hands over to the left foot and repeat on that side. Return to the center and stretch here once again taking another deep breath to more thoroughly loosen the hips. If you are working on your splits this is an ideal time to work on that position (Figure 7.26–7.27).

7.26

7.27

Slowly raise the torso and keep the feet wide with the toes pointed forward. Adjust the feet in such a way that you can shift the center and torso over to the right by bending the right leg and straightening the left leg. Only go as far as is possible while keeping the soles of both feet on the ground (Figure 7.28). A small but important detail here is to keep the toes of each foot pointing forward as much as possible without too much turn out. Repeat on the other side with the feet in the same orientation. Next repeat the same initial position on the right side only now point the left toes to the ceiling, balancing on the left heel (Figure 7.29). Repeat this new position on the other side as well. These positions further loosen the hips, ankles, and improve balance.

7.28

7.29

7.30

7.31

7.32

Bring the body back to center with the feet remaining wide. Pivot on the balls of the feet so that the body now faces 90 degrees to the right. The body should now be in a lunge with the front right leg bent at 90 degrees and the left rear leg as straight as possible. The sole of the right foot is on the floor with the knee of the right leg being no farther than above the instep of the right foot. The ball of the left foot is on the floor with the heel remaining up. Square the hips to the new direction and sink the hips down to increase the stretch to the hip flexor at the top of the left quadriceps. Now twist the torso to the right and take the left tricep, place it outside of the right thigh, place the palms of the hands together, and hold the twist. Breathe deeply in this position to further stretch the hip flexor as well as the musculature around the spine and right hip (Figure 7.30–7.32).

After releasing the palms, place them on the floor next to the lead foot and bring the knee of the rear leg gently to the floor. Support most of the weight with the hands on the floor as the hips shift forward. The right knee should now be past the toes. Typically this is a dangerous position for the knee to hold when standing. This is an unsupported position and any weight and force while standing will put undue stress on the ligaments of the knee. With the palms of the hands supporting the weight of the body however, the structures of the knee and ankle can be exercised without putting undue strain on them (Figure 7.33).

7.33

Step the lead foot to the rear to meet the back foot. Press both palms into the floor and push the hips towards the ceiling while straightening the legs and keeping the soles of the feet on the floor. This position is commonly called "downward facing dog" in yoga practice (Figure 7.34). It is a great stretch for the back, shoulders, and hamstrings simultaneously. Hold this position for at least 20 seconds. Afterwards alternate rolling through the feet from the ball to the heel and further stretch out the belly of the calf muscles (Figure 7.35).

7.34

7.35

Finally walk the hands back to the feet folding the body at the waist. Let the body relax and bend the knees to initiate a roll up the spine, stacking each vertebra on top of each other until the head finally floats to the top of the spine arriving in a relaxed and available standing position.

There are many ways to warm up. No one sequence is the be-all, end-all way to warm up, although some warm-ups prepare the body better for some work than others. Also, you may find that some of the positions are more difficult to maintain for your particular body than others. Feel free to spend a bit longer on these areas but try not to neglect other exercises that may seem easier to manage. Regardless, no matter how much or how little time you have to work, train, and rehearse in a given session always make time for warming up. Preparing yourself for the work in this way will allow you to be more fit, less injury-prone, and in a better place to improve skills more quickly. This is where your body, your breathing, and your mind will begin to coalesce in the common quest for the work ahead of you.

CHAPTER 8

Partnered Conditioning

After warming up, a good regimen of strength conditioning can be useful to improve muscle tone and further develop coordination. If alone, a performer can do a series of solitary exercises such as push-ups, planks, burpees (squat-thrusts,) and sit-ups. However, theatre is a collaborative art and is at its best when people come together to be in the same space at the same time. To further cultivate the collaborative spirit of the performing artist, the following are a series of partnered strengthening exercises that should be done with a partner. Most of these exercises I learned originally from Kyle Rowling, a fight director and head of the Sydney Stage Combat School in Sydney, Australia. Over the years I have discovered some other partnered exercises as well, which has lengthened the list. I find opportunities to perform these partnered exercises with a fellow artist or scene partner whenever I can so I can better gauge my physical responses to external energy. The more opportunities performers have to partner with each other, no matter what the exercise, the more deftly they will be able to respond to each other's energy when engaged in training, rehearsal, or performance. What follows is a comprehensive offering of strength conditioning exercises to be done with your partner. A light workout for this sequence would be 10 repetitions of each move. A more vigorous workout would entail 30 repetitions. These repetitions may be performed at a quick pace with high reps or a slow pace with low reps. When one partner finishes a set, the partners should switch roles. Even though one partner will be performing the reps at a time the other partner should be working on proper positioning and alignment. Whatever the exercise, make sure to be in verbal communication with your partner so that the resistance given or the position supported is appropriate for you to perform the exercise to the best of your ability.

THE IRON CROSS

Stand in front of your partner facing away from him or her. One partner places his or her hands on the wrists of the partner facing away. Make certain not to grab the wrists. Simply place the open palms on top of the wrists. The partner facing away will raise the arms up from the sides so that both arms stretch out sideways until they are parallel to the floor. While this movement is being executed, the partner standing behind provides resistance. Once the arms are level with the shoulders and parallel to the floor the position can be relaxed and the arms can return to the original position at the sides. The muscles of the shoulder are worked during this exercise (Figures 8.1–8.2).

8.1   8.2

DECLINE PUSH-UPS

8.3

One partner gets on all fours (hands and knees table-top position) with a flat back. The other partner places his or her shins on either the hips or the upper back of the partner on all fours. Make certain not to throw the shins on to the lower back of the first partner since the lumbar region is unsupported in this position. The second partner then assumes a push-up position with a flat back and the eyes gazing towards the floor so that the entire spine is in alignment. In this position do as many push-ups as desired. This exercise targets the pectoral muscles (Figure 8.3).

PUSH-DOWNS

8.4

8.5

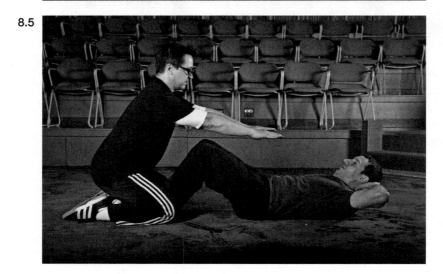

One partner assumes a sit-up position with the knees bent. The other partner kneels at the feet of the first partner puts the feet of the first partner between the knees of the second partner. As the first partner executes a sit-up and reaches the apex of the position, the second partner pushes the first partner back down to the floor by placing the hands on the upper pectorals of the first partner and extending the arms. The first partner should engage the abdominals on the way down as well so as not to slam the back into the floor (Figures 8.4–8.5).

LEG THROW-DOWNS

One partner lies on the floor in the supine position while the other partner stands at the head of the first partner. The feet of the standing partner should straddle the head of the supine partner. The supine partner holds on to the back of the standing partner's legs while raising the legs to meet the hands of the standing partner. The standing partner then throws the legs of the supine partner either forward, to the left, or to the right in a random pattern. The abdominals of the supine partner should remain engaged, the legs should be straight, and the feet should not be allowed to crash into the floor (Figures 8.6–8.7).

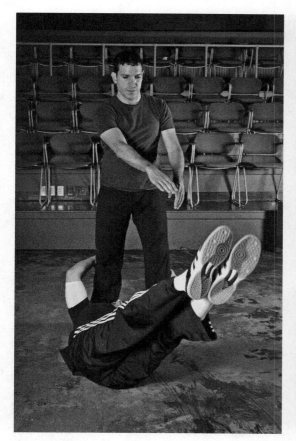

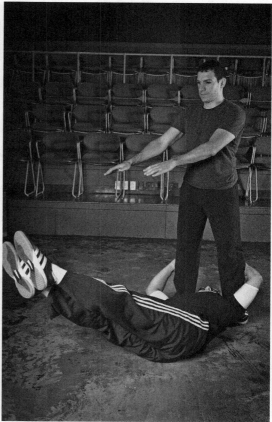

8.6   8.7

PARTNER PULL-UPS

One partner lies on the floor in the supine position. The other partner stands over the torso of the supine partner facing the head. Both partners grasp each other's forearms. The standing partner should have his or her knees slightly bent and his or her feet should be just underneath the armpits of the supine partner. Also, the standing partner should have his or her shoulders back and head up. Be careful not to round the back so as to maintain a strong position while the supine partner executes a pull-up. The pull-up can be done by lifting the whole body off the ground while balancing on the heels with the legs straight. A variation of this exercise can be done with the legs and hips on the floor while executing the pull-up with only the torso. This exercise targets the biceps and major muscles of the back for the partner performing the pull-ups while the standing partner works on alignment and balance (Figures 8.8–8.9).

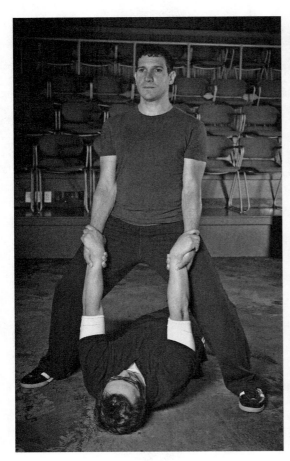

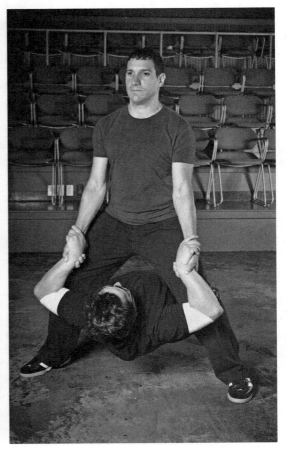

8.8   8.9

PARTNER DIPS

8.10

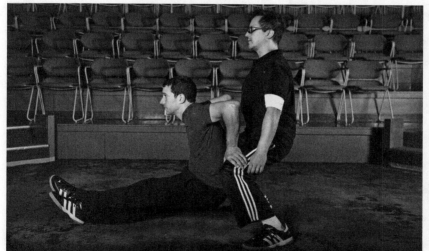

8.11

One partner assumes a low squat. The other partner gasps the quadriceps of the squatting partner while extending the legs and balancing on the heels. The partner with the legs extended then bends the arms and executes a dip as far as the range of motion will allow. The squatting partner should remain balanced throughout the exercise. If balance is difficult to maintain, the squatting partner can put his or her back against a wall to aid in the exercise. This exercise works the triceps of the partner performing the dips while also working the legs and balance of the partner squatting (Figures 8.10–8.11).

JUMP SPLITS

One partner lies in the supine position with the legs extended and the hands under the hips. The lower back should be flat on the floor and the legs should be lifted off the ground so as to engage the abdominals. The other partner stands to one side of the supine partner's legs facing in the opposite direction. As the supine partner opens the legs in a wide V-shape, the standing partner jumps in between the now separated legs. As the supine partner closes the legs, the standing partner continues jumping in the same direction to the other side. Timing is important as the jumping partner should take care not to land on the legs of the supine partner. Repeat the action back and forth until the desired number of repetitions is reached. This exercise works core strength, rhythm, and timing for both partners (Figures 8.12–8.14).

8.12

8.13

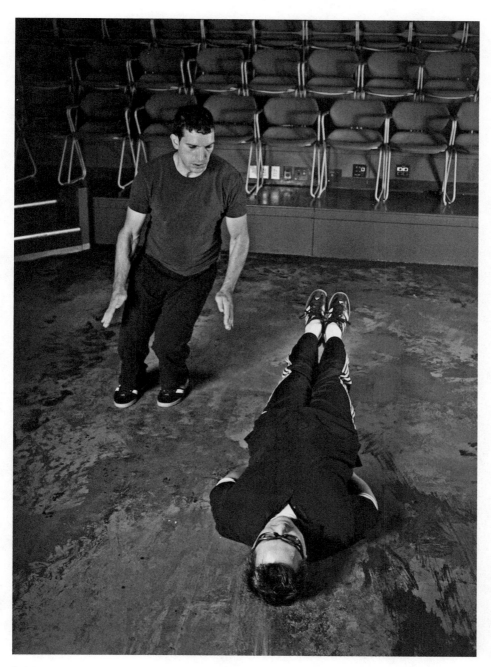

8.14

BACK BOARDS

One partner assumes a lunge position making certain the front knee does not move past the instep of the front foot. The sole of the rear foot is placed completely on the floor. The arms are stretched out straight and in front with the elbows down, palms facing out, fingers pointing to the ceiling. The other partner is in front, his or her back to the lunging partner with the arms parallel to the floor, bent 90 degrees at the elbow, palms facing down. Balancing on the heels, the standing partner leans back slightly keeping the body straight and the core engaged while placing the triceps against the flat palms of the lunging partner. The standing partner now works the muscles of the back (particularly the rhomboids and trapezius muscles) by articulating the arms forward until the tips of the fingers touch. Then articulate the arms to the rear as though the elbows could touch behind the back. All the while the body should remain straight with the hips in line with the shoulders. Be careful not to bend at the waist or round the spine excessively. Also an important point is that the lunging partner should be pushing towards the moving partner with straight outstretched arms. Bending the arms of the lunging partner will often result in a failure in the structure. The skeletal structure of the lunging partner should provide the base for the other partner to perform the exercise. As a result the lunging partner works on alignment and balance (Figures 8.15–8.17).

8.15

8.16

8.17

TABLE JUMPS

One partner gets on all fours (hands and knees table-top position) while the other partner stands to one side with palms placed on the upper back of the first partner near the scapula or shoulder blades. The second partner proceeds to jump over the hips and back to the opposite side of the tabled partner. The feet should leave the floor simultaneously, be raised so as to clear the partner's back as much as possible, and then return to the floor simultaneously as well. If this proves difficult, one may adjust the exercise to jump just clearing the partner's back one foot at a time. This exercise works the abdominal and leg muscles of the partner jumping and develops structural stability for the partner providing the base (Figures 8.18–8.20).

8.18

8.19

8.20

ASSISTED HANDSTAND PUSH-UPS

One partner assumes a static handstand position with the second partner grasping the ankles of the first partner. The hand-standing partner should have his or her head, shoulders, hips, and legs as vertical as possible with no bend or sway in the spine. The hand-standing partner bends the elbows until the top of the head touches the floor. Then the hand-standing partner extends the arms until they are straight. If the partner executing the push-ups needs help extending the arms, the partner at the ankles assists by pulling the first partner back to the original position. Take care that the spine (neck or back) of the hand-standing partner does not get out of alignment at any time. Also take care that the hand-standing partner stays in one location and does not begin to "walk" on the hands while performing the exercise. This exercise works the arm and shoulder muscles of both partners while developing alignment awareness and balance for the hand-standing partner (Figures 8.21–8.22).

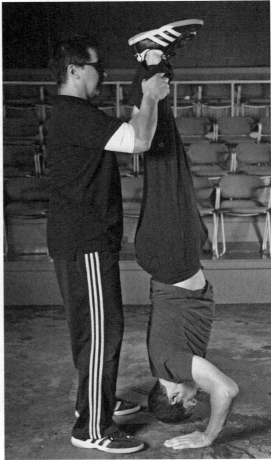

8.21

8.22

TABLE BACKSTRETCH

8.23

8.24

Take care to perform this partnered stretch with two partners of a similar build. One partner gets in the tabletop position while the other partner positions his or her hips to the side of the first partner's oblique muscles, right in the space between the first partner's hips and lower ribs. Keeping the hips to the side of the partner, the second partner bends backwards so that the lower back of the second partner's back is lying across the level lower back of the tabled partner. Once a comfortable position has been attained, the partner on top extends the arms over the head while the lower partner initiates spinal curves in both directions (often referred to as "Cat" and "Cow.") Perform these spinal isolations very slowly so as not to put undue stress on the lower back. This exercise provides not only a wonderful stretch of the back muscles for the top partner but also helps develop core strength for the tabled partner on the bottom (Figures 8.23–8.24).

STANDING BACKSTRETCH

Another backstretch can be done this time in the standing position. Here both partners begin by facing each other. One partner grasps the wrists of the other partner. The partner whose wrists are being grasped is being stretched. While the wrists of the second partner are being grasped both partners turn in the same direction so that they are both now facing away from each other with their arms over their heads (Figure 8.25). The partner who is doing the grasping then bends his or her legs so that the hips of the other partner are firmly placed in the small of the grasping partner's back (Figure 8.26). Then, the grasping partner bends forward slowly while extending the legs, stretching the arms forward, and lifting the other partner off the floor (Figure 8.28). Be certain to extend the legs here and not bend them

8.25

8.26

further. Bending the legs further will force the muscles to work more to keep the other partner up. This will quickly fatigue the legs. Extending the legs will allow the alignment of the skeletal structure to provide more support for the partner being stretched. If the stretch feels stable, the partners may wish to release the grip and relax even further into the stretch. When the partners wish to conclude the stretch, the bottom partner squeezes the wrists of the top partner and slowly tips back to the standing position. Without letting go both partners turn in the same direction so that they end in the same position they started in. It is important to end in this way in order to protect the lower back. This exercise stretches the muscles surrounding the spine, develops balance, and increases sensitivity to weight sharing for both partners.

8.27

8.28

These exercises are meant to help with good muscular maintenance for the major muscle groups most used in executing techniques. They also should begin to develop the physical partnering skills of each individual. After a while, each partner will begin to make physical adjustments naturally in relation to the other. Of course, there is no substitution for verbal communication. When in doubt, always talk to your partner.

CHAPTER 9

Combat Games

Games seem to be everywhere nowadays. They aren't just for playing on the field or to be watched on the television. Games are in our homes, on our computers, and on our phones. They are with us everywhere. Why the fascination? Why play games? The first and I hope most obvious answer is that games are fun. Or at least they should be fun. But why talk about games in the context of violence for stage and film? Is not everything pre-planned and choreographed much like the lines that the performers say? In this way fight choreography is not dissimilar to learning the lines of the script. The performer knows what words to say and what movements to do weeks before a performance. Hopefully he or she has practiced and rehearsed these exact words and movements many times. However, particularly in the case of live theatre, sometimes things do not go as planned. The rehearsed words or moves do not happen as intended. Most performers have the training to cover or improvise when this happens with words. But what about when it happens with fight choreography? If the performers are only versed in the exact moves of the altercation and not necessarily the concepts behind them, any interruption to the flow of the choreography will most likely grind to a halt. There will be no improvising because the performers do not have the training or the skill to adjust. This grinds not only the fight but also the entire production to a halt. This cannot happen. The show, as someone once famously said, must go on.

Developing and playing games, particularly ones that build skills and reinforce concepts tied to the art of acting and theatrical violence, enables the performer to adapt to real-time situations in performance. This allows the performer to be more in the moment and truly sensitive to the action rather than re-enacting a pre-determined sequence of moves. There is no doubt that learning choreography, a set pattern of physical moves, is a skill that any performer must acquire with proficiency. But this cannot be the sole purpose of presenting violence on stage. It has no soul, no possibility, nothing beyond simply choreography. There must be something more for the actor. Games allow the actor to make connections, both physical and conceptual, between executing choreography and bringing that choreography to life in performance.

The following games are for two people. I will refer to these people as "players" because that is what they should be doing with each other. Playing. The intention of each game will switch between competitive and cooperative but the essence of play should stay intact throughout.

PUSH AND RELEASE

The first time I remember playing this game was at the University of Toowoomba in Queensland, Australia. It was in a class taught by Tony Wolf for the Paddy Crean Workshop organized by the International Order of the Sword and Pen. It is also one of the first games I introduce to a group of actors when trying to get to know what their habitual patterns of movement are. It also provides a window into a person's attitude towards combative or competitive physical interactions with another person.

Both players start by facing each other in a neutral stance. The feet should be parallel to each other and at least shoulder-width apart with the knees bent. Players with dance training might think of this initial position as second position in deep plié. Players with a martial arts background could assume a horse stance or riding stance. The players get close enough to each other so that each player can touch the palms of the other. The arms of each player should be bent and not outstretched. The beginning of this game is cooperative. Both players play with sharing weight only through the contact in the palms (Figure 9.1). The feet should remain in place. Players should feel free to explore their shared mobility through the arms, torso, hips, and knees as they move in response to each other. This is also a nice way to gently warm up the muscles and joints and also make contact with another player.

Then, at a mutually and verbally agreed upon moment, the game becomes competitive. The goal of this game is to create an imbalance in the other player so that one or both feet move from their initial starting position without losing one's own balance. This can only be accomplished through the player connectivity in the palms. A player may choose to push through the palms of the other player to create this imbalance (Figure 9.2). If, however, one player elects to push and the other player senses the push, the second player may release the contact in an attempt to get the first player off-balance (Figure 9.3). As a result there are two ways to be successful and win at the game – Push or Release. Exactly when a player elects to use either tactic is entirely up to him or her. Keep in mind that if a player releases the contact between player palms and no one is off balance, the contact is immediately initiated once again. A running tally is kept during the course of the game to see how many times one player can get the other player off-balance. If a player bends over Matrix-style but maintains his or her foot position then no point is scored.

9.1

9.2

9.3

After the first round, ask yourself the question, "What technique was most successful for me? Push or release?" Ask the other players in the group the same. There will be some people who find that pushing yields better results for them. Others will notice that they tried to find more opportunities for releasing and letting the energy of their partners carry them off balance. It's a binary situation. Nearly 95% of people fall into one of the two camps. Perhaps 5% of players will use the techniques of pushing and releasing equally but these are rare. The first thing to do is notice what your natural default mode is for playing a competitive or combative game with someone. Do you like to push or release? Do you like to make the first move or do you prefer to respond to what someone else does first? Do you like sending energy out and away from you into another body or so you prefer to receive energy and turn it to your advantage? There is no one way better than another. Ask yourself these questions honestly and answer them without judgment.

Typically I find in a group of actors there are more release players than push players. Actors, particularly ones who have elected to take classes to further their training, have cultivated the ability to respond very well to situations. They tend to defer to the wishes of others whether that is the instructor, a new scene partner, a fellow classmate, or a director. They are good at taking direction. It doesn't matter where the direction comes from, or if it's physical or conceptual. Actors have developed this ability to negotiate the business of performing. It shows up even in the classroom setting. This is not something that should be judged or criticized but it should be recognized because it leads to physical tendencies in the body that should be acknowledged.

Once you have identified your tendency play the game again with the same partner and see if you can find opportunities to be successful at the game by making the choice you didn't habitually default to in the first round. If you are a Push person, find opportunities to release. If you are a Release person, look for places to push. This doesn't mean the players don't still use the tactics that worked for each of them initially. Each player simply tries to utilize his or her respective non-habitual choice to make the game more unpredictable.

Once you have played round two trying to make the non-habitual choice with the same partner change partners if you can. Go immediately into the competitive version of Push and Release. The next person you meet may be smaller than you, or taller, or have longer arms, or stronger legs than you. Whether you are conscious of it or not you will be sizing up your opponent to see what tactics you will use to win at the game. You will probably wonder from the other player's physical stature and build if he or she is a Push person or a Release person. But how do you really know? You won't know unless you play with them. By playing the game a player gets to know the tendencies, patterns, and behavior of the other player. And the more you play the game with different players the more you will get to know your own tendencies, patterns, and behavior when put in this particular situation. The act of playing the game allows the players to find out about themselves and about each other. When you and I play, I start to know more about myself because you start to know more about yourself. We help each other know.

There are of course some pitfalls. Some players will be reluctant to play the game fully and to win. This will be manifested in a few ways. When they are trying to push they will indicate this to their partner by leaning in and shifting their centers forward in front of their point of balance. A receptive opponent will pick up on this and simply release. Some less observant players may just lean-push back creating a stalemate. The game becomes boring when force meets force over and over. This would be the equivalent of a scene where two characters shout at each other over and over. The actors feel like they are expending a lot of energy but the situation goes nowhere.

Another form of indicating is when a player prepares to push. The shoulders rising up and the hands actually moving back towards the player doing the push before extending to the opponent whom the player is trying to push off-balance exhibit this. This going back-to-go-forward motion is not rooted in a desire to play the game but be "nice" to the other player by announcing the intent to push. Again, observant opponents will simply release and score a point by letting the pusher put themselves off-balance. Of course this is a severe handicap to the player preparing to push. It is also very boring to play against or even watch this player because we know what the player is going to do before he or she does it. That's not very exciting is it? The best players don't prepare to push or release. They simply do the action. This makes the game more impulsive, surprising, and more interesting to play and watch.

The goal of the game is to get the opponent off-balance. The way a human body becomes off-balance is when the center of gravity goes beyond the equilibrium point provided by the orientation of the feet. You may notice that when some players push they stop their push a few inches in front of the space where the body of their opponent is. This also becomes a handicap to the player pushing. The full effect of the push cannot be realized unless the arms of the player initiating the push are fully extended past the center of the opponent. Stopping short results in, at best, a tickle and not a push. Another form of the not-push is when the direction of the push does not travel through the palms directly towards the body of the opponent. Rather you may see the push flaring out to the sides as if the player doing the push is waving the air away that surrounds the opponent. If we truly want to win at the game, we would attempt to initiate a change in the balance of the other player by affecting the positive space of their body rather than the negative space around it.

A typical game lasts 3 minutes. Shorter games can be played but I find that the longer games allow for more opportunities for strategy and deep physical listening.

FINGER FENCING

Finger fencing is a great game I also first learned from Tony Wolf, and then was reintroduced to when studying fencing at Bay State Fencers in Somerville, MA. While this game may seem more suited as training for swordplay it actually has more applications for tactile kinesthetic response, since the game is played through constant contact.

The players take either their right or left hands (a matter of preference) and clasp them in what I call the "buddy clasp." It's not a handshake position where the thumbs are on top but rather a clasping of the hands where the fingers are on top. This should put the hands in

9.4

9.5

a position to extend the index fingers straight out so that they point to the other player (Figure 9.4). I suggest accompanying the extension of the index finger with a sound effect to signal a strong start to the game. I find "SHING!" works quite nicely. The players stay connected through the duration of the game. The goal is to score a touch on the other player's body without being scored on (Figures 9.6–9.7). The entire body is fair game excluding sensitive areas and the face for what I hope are obvious reasons. Players should move each other around to take advantage of angles and positioning to score a touch. Each game should be played for 2 minutes. I think you'll find that 2 minutes is more than enough to work up a good sweat.

9.6

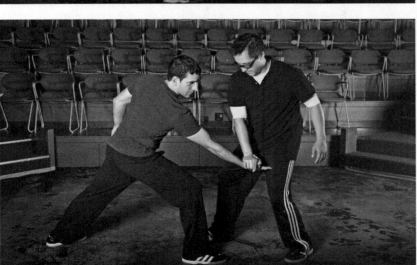

9.7

This is a competitive game where the score is continually tallied through the 2 minutes. Initially new players will most likely simply try to overpower each other. As they fatigue and realize that it is nearly impossible to blast through the other's defenses, the players will naturally start to circle each other trying to look for opportunities and openings to score touches. This will bring awareness particularly to the lower half of the body where the legs become vulnerable targets. As more attempts are made to score on the legs, this will oblige each player to be more agile with their feet, moving not only the individual, but also the other player through the space more vigorously through the course of the game.

Players will find that if they are really trying to score a touch and really trying not to be touched then both players will range about the playing space quite a bit. It also brings spatial awareness of the players as a unit to the fore. Playing this game in a group is even more challenging because all of the couples must play the game and play to win without crashing into other couples. Later on, when mass battles, rumbles, and bar fights are studied, this is a good introduction to group awareness in a violent, combative context.

WEIGHT SHARE: THE SHAPE OF CONFLICT

There are two weight share games that I enjoy very much and are simple ways to initiate contact with a partner. They are great games to reinforce trust and kinesthetic response at a slower tempo.

I played this game for the first time at summer camp. The two players stand back to back. The goal is for both to lower themselves to the ground slowly by leaning into each other without using their hands or speaking. The final position is typically the two players sitting back to back with their knees bent. I, however, enjoy sliding the hips out at this point more and more, again without the use of the hands, until both players are lying supine or face up with their heads resting side by side on each other's shoulder. The players should then attempt to get back up in the same manner, leaning into each other without speaking. In order to get back to the seated position, the hands may be used. But getting from the seated position to standing should require no hands at all. If you are wearing socks you may find this difficult as the feet will tend to slip out from underneath the more you lean into your partner.

It is a classic cooperative weight share where both players must work together wordlessly to move in a controlled manner without crashing back to the ground. The secret lies in the amount of weight one gives the other person. Give too much and your partner gets overwhelmed and crunched into the fetal position. Give too little and you get overwhelmed yourself. The players must find the perfect combination of force and weight to put into each other. The more surface area connection each player feels along the back the more likely they will be relying on each other to keep from crashing down. Just the right amount of force each way will result in both bodies moving steadily towards the floor or away from it.

Another variation of this weight share I played many times in acting school, mostly in my movement classes. In this variation both players face each other and stand toe to toe.

9.8

9.9

9.10

9.11

9.12

The players grasp each other gently, one right hand to the partner's left forearm and the left hand to the partner's right forearm. Very slowly the partners lean back and extend their arms. Eventually, both players' arms should be straight with only the slightest necessary muscular tension present to keep holding on to the other person. The players should feel as though if either person let go then both would fall to the floor (Figures 9.8–9.11).

Even though the games are cooperative by nature one could easily see how these shapes could be used in a violent interaction. In the first game two bodies are pushing into each other. In the non-cooperative version of this we might imagine that one person is trying to dislodge another from a location or position in order to gain a dominant advantage. In the second game the two bodies are pulling at each other. Here we may imagine a competitive interaction where one person is trying to make another person move to a certain point. In either event, it is a moment of possibility where something is on the verge of change. If you look closely, notice what kind of shape is made during each of these weight-share exercises. The size of the shape changes but it is always there in one form or another. The easiest way to see it is during the second exercise, face-to-face, with the arms outstretched and relaxed. If the players' bodies are of a similar size you will find a perfect equilateral triangle. Look for the triangle again in the other exercises, or when the position of the bodies changes throughout the exercise. The type, location, or number of each triangle might change but the triangle will always be present.

Triangles are the structure of change, or heat, of motion. In science and mathematics the symbol "delta" is a triangle and signifies change. In chemistry a compound structure that is triangular in shape is nearly always transitional and is always looking to transition to a more stable structure. We can see this in human bodies. Two football players on the gridiron run towards each other. Their upper bodies press forward and gather momentum. At the moment of impact a triangle is made, each body leaning into the other on impact.

Performers should be sensitive to whether or not they are making the correct shapes on stage to represent the violence. If the actors' bodies are fully upright and parallel to each other a square or rectangle exists between them. Even if they hurl invectives at each other there will be little threat of violence unless the space between them changes. A triangle must be created. If none exists the audience will perceive that there is no real conflict between the characters. The sides must either collapse or expand for the interaction to go anywhere.

DRUNKEN SAILORS

This is a cooperative game that combines elements of the previous weight sharing exercise as well as the finger fencing game. Both partners should begin in the same "buddy clasp" position as in finger fencing (Figure 9.13). The partners should decide who is going to move forward first and who will move backward. The partner moving forward should follow the lead of the partner moving backward (Figure 9.14). The partner moving back should walk slowly at first and use the counter-balance of the partner moving forward to gently move to the ground in the supine position (Figure 9.15). When done properly and with balanced control the partner going to the ground should not have to use the other hand to touch the floor. In fact, this game should develop a habit of not having to use the hands at all when descending to the floor. Once one partner is lying on the ground, the other partner now begins to walk backward helping the first partner up off the floor. The partner now walking backward is leading the motion and continues to walk back until the other partner is up and walking forward. Now the exercise is repeated for the other partner. As the game continues the partners may wish to increase their tempo. As the tempo increases the partners should begin making sounds as though they were intoxicated sailors on a boat that is listing side to side. If the game is going really well the partners may elect to change the directions after each turn. This game will start to develop the physical and vocal actions involved in the techniques where the performers go to the ground.

9.13

9.14

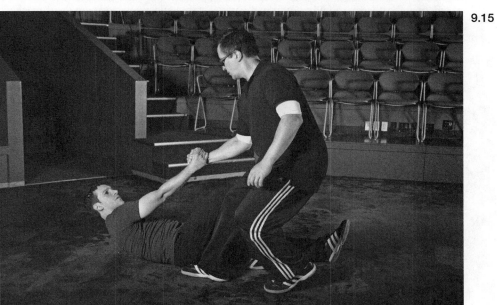

9.15

PUSHING HANDS

This is a game that follows from an exercise I first learned when studying Long Fist and White Crane Gongfu and Tai Chi at YMAA with Dr. Yang, Jwing-Ming. The traditional exercise is used for students to experientially investigate principles used in martial arts such as timing, centering, coordination, and sensitivity. Different schools may have their own flavor of how to conduct the pushing hands exercise. The following is just one suggestion of a sequence to an activity that I have found incredibly useful in physical training for the performer.

Essentially this version of pushing hands is a game of leading and following. It is a cooperative game where both players strive for a deeper, more significant physical interaction rather than one player simply trying to keep up with the other. Both players start the game in a closed stance; both right foot forward or left foot forward. The outside of each player's lead foot should be flush up against the other player's lead foot. Whichever side or foot is forward, raise the corresponding lead arm so that the back of one player's lead forearm or wrist contacts the back of the wrist or forearm of the other player (Figure 9.16). It is decided verbally between the two players who will lead and who will follow. The objective of the game is simply to maintain the contact between the arms *at all times*. The leader will begin by simply and slowly moving his or her arm in any direction he or she chooses without displacing the feet. The follower will simply follow the movements dictated by the leader (Figure 9.17). Both players are responsible for maintaining the contact. Try to experiment with moving in as many directions in space as is possible with your partner without losing the contact. If the contact is disrupted at any time the players should reset from the initial starting position and begin the game again (Figures 9.18–9.19).

9.16

9.17

9.18

9.19

After some time the follower may be tired of following. At any time the person who is following can take leadership of the interaction by giving a clear physical motion with the arm that is not already in contact with the partner. The follower should sweep the arm in a wide, arcing fashion intercepting the partner's arm that is already in contact with the player (Figure 9.20). Again, there should be no moment when the players are ever not in physical contact with each other. As a result, the moment of interception will actually have three arms in contact before the follower takes the arm that has already been more active in the exercise away. Once the exchange has been made then whoever was following is now leading and whoever was leading is now following. Changes of leadership can happen at any time.

Some things to consider: try to let the movement start at a slower pace and then build in tempo as the interaction between the players deepens. If the contact is lost, then you know

9.20

9.21

9.22

9.23

you have gone too fast for the interaction and the players should begin the game again in the initial starting position at their slowest shared pace.

Once a good connectivity has been established, one player who is leading may elect to start moving his or her feet so that both bodies now become mobile (Figure 9.21). By utilizing the topography and dimensions of the space with the now mobile unit, the two players can more freely explore the horizontal extension and vertical level possibilities of their shared physical system. They can see how high they can reach to the ceiling together or how their bodies interact on the floor (Figures 9.22–9.23). Anything is possible as long as the physical point of contact remains constant.

Something to consider: do you like leading or following or both equally? Most actors I meet enjoy following much more than leading. Whatever your preference play the game again, except this time look for more opportunities to engage with the part of the game you don't gravitate towards as much. If you like to lead, try following longer. If you like to follow, try to take the lead more often. See if and how this changes the game and your interaction with your partner. Regardless, remember what your proclivity is. It is good information to know what role of leading or following we typically default to.

OCULAR FOCUS (AKA EYE-CONTACT)

Once the players have played this game for a few minutes they should now draw their attention to their focus. Where were they looking? Typically when people new to Pushing Hands play in this way, they keep their eyes on the point of contact, in this case the wrists or forearms. This makes sense as a person will use sight to get extra information about the point of contact and its location in space in relation to his or her partner. But we already have the sense of touch giving us information through the physical contact. Do the players need to rely so heavily on looking at the point of contact to actually respond to each other?

Try the exact same exercise keeping all of the guidelines listed above. The only difference this time is the players should start the game by looking anywhere but the point of contact. The players can look at the fan on the ceiling or a speck of dust on the floor or the knee of the other partner – anywhere but the point of contact at the wrist. Players should make sure that they have a specific and exact point of focus.

There can be a tendency in this part of the exercise to shift into "soft-focus" where the eyes are not looking anywhere or focusing on anything in particular. Peripheral vision is an important ability to acknowledge. However, relying too much on this ability makes one's focus too general. By being in a constant state of soft-focus one ends up focusing on everything. And when one focuses on everything it is really a focus on nothing since all things in the world, or at least one's view, cannot and should not all have the same value. This is particularly true for performers on stage. We are in the business of showing an audience what is important and to do that we must make choices. The most basic of these choices is where to look and what to look at. If you look at something with interest then the audience will tend to follow suit. Peripheral vision and soft focus are useful. They open up our awareness to the things around us so that we can then *shift* focus when necessary. This should naturally happen in this variation of the game. The point of focus can shift as long as it never rests on the point of contact. Experiment with the distance you look away from your partner as well as the duration of time you look away. Try to experiment with extremes of both great and small distances from your partner and long and short time duration in settling on a point of focus.

For the next variation of this game begin again at the starting position. Keep the same guidelines but change the ocular focus yet again. Now the players should look into each other's eyes, holding eye contact for the duration of this next play. The eye contact should be fixed and never waver from the eyes. If the eyes of one player flit back to the wrist or down to the feet at any given time, the other player should immediately insist that the eye contact be re-established. One way to do this is for the follower to take over leadership immediately if the leader breaks eye contact. If the follower breaks eye contact then the leader can adjust his or her level to get right in front of the follower's eyes wherever they happen to wander. Yet another way is for one player to tell the other player who looks away, "Don't look away from me!" The players should feel free to turn it into a staring contest.

Typically players feel that the game shifts considerably when eye focus is changed, particularly when the focus is locked on the eyes. Notice how each change in focus changes your attitude towards your partner, the exercise, and the way in which you move.

SEEING WITHOUT SEEING

Now that the game has been played for a bit and if you and your partner are feeling comfortable in the rhythm and connectivity you have established you may be ready for the following variation. All of the guidelines are in place once again with regard to staying in constant contact, change of leadership, exploring levels, space, tempo, etc. The players begin at the starting position. This time *both* players close their eyes. It should go without saying that even if you feel a good connection with your partner, please start this variation of the game slowly and far away from any sharp objects or high cliffs. Do, however, try to do this in a space where other players are playing the same game. This aspect of the game can be the most frightening and exhausting but also the most fun. The other senses of the body become ultra-sensitive when sight is deprived and the body is in motion. Be sure the pace with your partner is manageable, take sure steps, and use the off-hand that is not connected to your partner as a "whisker" to feel the space around you and avoid possible collisions with tables, walls, or other people.

If having both partners without sight proves too much too soon, the game can also be played where only one partner closes his or her eyes. Try this exercise in both ways where the leader has his or her eyes open and the follower has his or her eyes closed or vice versa to experience the different effects sightlessness has on leading and following.

Now that you have experienced each version of Pushing Hands you can shift freely using all of the variations you have explored so far in a single play. Partners should keep exploring and experimenting with physicality through constant contact while also shifting through all of the possibilities for ocular focus. Note that each partner can choose what to focus on individually in his or her own time. One partner may be focusing on the point of contact while the other partner is focusing on the chair across the room. Or one partner may be focusing his or her eyes on the other partner while that partner has his or her eyes closed. Feel free to play with as many variations as possible but never lose the specificity of ocular focus.

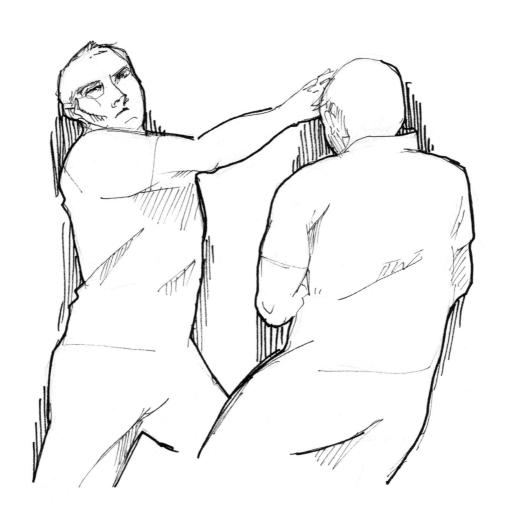

PART IV

PROCESS AND PERFORMANCE

CHAPTER 10

The Violent Soundscape

In order for the human body to make sound there must be effort. The diaphragm lowers to make room for the lungs to expand with air. When enough air is present in the lungs the diaphragm rises to expel the air up through the trachea to pass over the vocal folds and create sound. That sound then passes through the oropharynx and becomes formed through the manipulations of the tongue and lips. This is an over simplification of the process that happens when a person wishes to speak. Moreover, there are many steps between the will to speak and the act of speaking. Speaking is just that: an act. It takes effort through action of multiple parts of the human body in order to make sound. It takes even more parts added to that in order for that sound to become intelligible. Add to this that sound can convey not only information but also feeling. The things that we say have meaning but when communicating with each other it becomes more and more clear that oftentimes it is not what we say that has the greatest effect but *how* we say it that ultimately carries the day.

Creating violent sounds follows the same path. We not only want to communicate information, typically the information that something was struck, but also the sense of the effect of that strike not only physically but emotionally as well.

THE KNAP

Taking the knap in theatre is a bit different than it is in the everyday. Although actors have been known to take more than one nap on the cot in the greenroom during a 10-out-of-12 tech, taking a knap (pronounced the same as "nap" as the "k" is silent) during a scene is to provide a sound to add dimension to a moment of violence.

Merriam-Webster lists the word "knap" as being first used sometime in the fifteenth century and defines it as a noun to be "a crest of a hill or summit" and also as a verb "to rap, snap, or break with a quick blow; especially to shape (as flints) by breaking off pieces." The etymology of "knap" as it applies to the theatrical definition is still in contention. The "knap" or "knapping" is the technique used in performance to simulate the sound of violent contact when in fact no actual contact is made. Knaps are made primarily as a percussive slap of one hand against the other (clap knap), one hand against an area of one's own body (body knap), or one hand against an object or partner (partnered or shared knap). We can quickly see the relation of the theatrical definition to the word in its original use as a verb. The appearance of "quick blow" in the second definition strongly links to the theatrical use through violent contact. Instead of applying it to pieces of flint we apply it to hands or body parts in performance.

Oftentimes when studying techniques, especially ones that rely heavily on extreme physicality, we can be so concerned with how something looks or feels in our own body that we forget how the moment sounds and what kind of feeling it engenders in anyone observing. Without fail, an observer will unconsciously and impulsively respond more suddenly to a movement accompanied by sound than to one without sound. If the sound is sharp, percussive, and loud, the response from the observer will be even more instinctively felt at the moment it happens. Why is this? Perhaps it has something to do with our hearing being connected to our mechanism for survival. If we imagine hunter-gatherer ancestors trying to survive on the plains, in the jungle, and on the steppes however many years ago, seeing any predator or possible life-threat would be most likely only during the daytime. But hearing danger, the rustle of the grass, the snarl of the animal, or even the clap of thunder before a storm, could be relied on at any time, day or night, barring any ancillary sounds that would conflict with hearing it. Sounds warn us of any imminent danger.

Let us not so quickly forget nor disregard the first original definition of "a crest of a hill or summit." This definition brings to mind images of a peak or zenith. In a way this definition can inform the way we approach knaps. Instead of thinking of the knap as ancillary, an afterthought, the final component to be layered on top of a technique, what if we treated the sound as the pinnacle of a violent moment? By focusing on the sound of impact made at the peak moment of violence we can more easily tap into this element that seems to affect an observing human so effectively – the mechanism of attaching sounds to danger and human survival. Making the sound of the knap central to the violence helps us create a full, multidimensional moment full of sound and fury and not just a moving picture.

If these knaps are that important how exactly do we make them? There are so many different ways to strike a human body and so many things to consider such as is the body part clothed, what is the velocity of the hit, is the strike with the hand or the foot? Any number of these questions and more must be answered to find the appropriate knap for each hit. We must become scientists and test our theories of what knap might be just right for any given hit. Creating the right knap for the right moment at the right time may very well be our version of the alchemist's Philosopher's Stone. This is the moment where we seek to turn a technique lead into gold.

Unlike the fabled Philosopher's Stone, however, there is not just one knap that will be the panacea for every hit we perform. If we were to take the three types of knaps listed earlier we can begin to group our knap techniques to more easily aid in our experimentation. Each of these three types of knaps can be modified in a variety of ways in order to produce the type of sound that seems most appropriate to the hit.

The type of sound we can produce, and therefore the effect we produce from the knap, hinges on two factors: volume and quality. If we consider the use of volume as a simple scale of 1–10 with 1 being nearly inaudible and 10 being the loudest single clap possible we can start to apply this to any violent moment. Typically the harder the hit, the louder the sound we expect to hear. Other factors such as clothing covering the weapon or target, size difference in attacker versus receiver, and intent of what the attacker means to do with the hit can factor in to how loud the hit should be.

In considering the quality of the sound produced by the knap we must be a bit more discerning. All the above questions must be answered to inform the quality of sound attached to the hit. How does a slap to the cheek sound different than a punch to the jaw? How does a knee to the stomach sound different than a kick to the groin? We must answer these questions honestly first.

Does this mean we actually take our friends and kick them in the groin and record the sound? Suffering for one's art is a common theme in the theatre and even accepted to a degree. But here we use one of our greatest human tools and one that most acting teachers, including Stanislavski, purported to be the actor's greatest asset: the imagination. Are we concerned with the reality of what a given strike may sound like? Yes. Should we try to get as close to that sound as possible? Absolutely. Should we actively injure our fellow actors in the process of discovering what that is? Not if we can help it. Like any good scientist we cannot experiment on each other in such a way that causes harm. Any good performance should be concerned with revealing truth – the truth of a story from all perspectives, the truth behind a relationship, the truth of the essence of any given moment. However, we should not be so much concerned with *literal* truth as much as we should be concerned with *theatrical* truth. This is an important distinction and one often lost among actors particularly those studying in drama school early in their careers. The literal truth to be anything that is undeniably true in the world and therefore is also true in the confines of the theatre – the chair that I sit on at the table in a scene is literally a chair in the world and that is how I am treating it on stage as well. However, if I create such conditions through the magic of theatre, through my imagination or with the help of some impressive lighting and a wizard of a props master, that chair may become a dragon that I must fight and vanquish. If I believe it is a dragon and for a few moments the audience believes that it is a dragon, then in terms of theatrical reality that chair has indeed become a dragon. Theatrical reality is what makes a performance become magical. In a theater we believe things to be true both performer and audience alike. For the greatest moments in performance both actor and audience share what the great acting teacher Sanford Meisner called "living truthfully in imaginary circumstances."

But now let us return to quality of sound. How do we make these various strikes sound different and unique one from the other? A list of each broad category follows with examples of each.

1 *The Clap Knap*

   This is the most common form of knap. The clap knap is, just as it sounds, performed by clapping the hands together. We can produce a host of different sounds with a simple clapping motion. Putting the base of the front of the digits of one hand into the palm of the other tends to produce the loudest most resonant sound. It's the same clap you would most likely use after a killer concert from your favorite band of all time. You will do this type of clap instinctively. The best track for the hands while performing this knap is vertically with the palm of the lower hand travelling up toward the digits of the higher hand. This allows for a greater chance of the body masking the movement of the hands during the knap. The only problem with the sound created by this knap is that it sounds just like that: a clap. If our aim is to make an observer believe that the hand has struck another body part other than another hand, most likely the cheek of the face, we may need to be more selective in the quality of the sound produced.

2 *The Body Knap*

   This knap is also quite common especially when employed to simulate contact to the head from a strike other than a slap. The most common use of the body knap is typically during a non-contact punch to the head. Body knaps can be made by slapping one hand against any part of the body. Obviously it is more comfortable to slap some parts of the body than others. The most comfortable and also resonant sounding knaps are typically made with the hand coming in contact with large muscle groups such as the upper pectorals (chest knap), the outside of the upper thigh (leg knap), or the latissimus dorsi (back knap). There are other sites for knapping as well such as the abdominal sheath, the inside or outside of the thigh, the gluteals, the back, even the upper arm or forearm. No matter what the location of the body knap, always endeavor to perform the knap with a relaxed hand to minimize self-injury. Relaxing the knap hand will not only minimize discomfort to the operator it will also maximize the likelihood of getting a louder, more resonant sound. Naturally, depending on the body composition of the performer some of these muscle groups may be more developed than others. The more muscle in a given area, the more resonant sound will be produced and the more comfortable and repeatable the particular knap technique will be for the performer. Sometimes, however, we may not want a particularly resonant sound for a strike because the hit should be played as a weak one, the target being struck does seem to demand such a loud sound be produced, or perhaps just for the sake of sound variation. In this instance bones, joints, and soft, sensitive tissue should be avoided so as not to self-inflict any injury. Additionally, bony bits and soft tissue will typically make less sound when struck in comparison to their more meaty counterparts.

3 *The Shared Knap*

   The shared knap can actually be either a clap knap or a body knap. The only difference is that it relies on both performers to make the sound. A high-five is an example of a shared knap. More particular examples of shared knaps can be found attached to certain moves in the techniques section.

4   *The Vocal Knap*

The vocal knap is a vocalization that is made by the receiver at the moment of contact to indicate a landed blow. This type of knap is often employed when for whatever reason the performer cannot make a suitably appropriate sound using the previous knap techniques. This may be the case because the costuming or staging prohibit the performer from easily executing a knap such as when the performer is holding an object with both hands. It is important to note here that the timing of the vocal is what makes this a knap technique. The appropriately voiced sound is made at the precise moment of perceived contact here, not afterwards as would be expected when any one of the other knaps are employed.

For examples of clap knaps and body knaps, see the companion website at www.focalpress.com/cw/najarian.

Make no mistake, getting a hearty, resonant, and logically appropriate sound for a given hit is the primary concern when performing knaps. If the knap doesn't make a sound that completes the picture of the hit then it may as well have been left out altogether. However, when practicing knaps with an eye towards performance there is an element that must be attended to that is often times over looked – how to mask the knap so that the technique of it is invisible to the audience. (Note for film – the performers in a fight scene for film will never have to knap. Ever. Sounds such as vocals will be recorded at the time of filming but the task of making the hits is left to another artist. The sounds of bodily contact, particularly strikes, will be added to the scene by the foley artist in post-production after filming. In the theater, however, the performer is responsible in the moment of the strike to make the perfect sound to sell the hit.)

We already have some staging techniques that will help make the knap less visible to the audience (see Chapter 11 The Illusion of Violence). However sometimes the interaction between performers cannot be staged in such a way as to conceal or camouflage the knaps. Knaps on their own are enough of an odd and unnatural motion that the hands often seize up during the technique becoming too stiff to look naturally part of a character's gestural life. To become proficient at any knap, the performer must release any stiffness and extraneous tension in the hands (this will also minimize the chance of the performer putting too much force into the knap, which may lead to self-injury). However, the hands cannot and should not be dead and lifeless hanging at the sides of the performer. If this were to happen then at the moment of the strike the very next movement of the hands would draw attention to the technique of the knap. Humans are animals after all and the eyes of all animals are instinctively drawn to notice sudden movement. If the hands go from a still and unoccupied position to a fast clap then the jig is up. The performer ceases to be a character living through a violent circumstance but rather is revealed as a performer who is executing a technique. This is precisely what should be avoided. In order to connect the technique to the reality of the moment the performer must rely on the ability of the hands to *gesture*.

A gesture is defined as "a movement or position of the hand, arm, body, head, or face that is expressive of an idea, thought, or emotion" (dictionary.com.) Since we are focusing particularly on the hands then they must be engaged with the particular task of expressing a particular idea at the moment right before the knap. The hands must be engaged in a gesture that is specific to the moment leading up to this particular moment of violence involving the knap. When the hands are engaged gesturally in this way the audience will cease to see an actor preparing for a technique. Rather they will simply see a character responding to an imminent threat.

Of course there are many gestural positions of the hands that could be explored and used depending on the scene. However, there are a few gestural positions for the hands to assume before a strike happens that maximize the possibility of getting a good knap.

- *Gesture #1*. Preparing for the clap knap: before the strike assume a gestural position with both hands in front of the torso with the palms facing each other as much as seems natural and comfortable. One hand should be a higher level than the other in order to keep a vertical track through the course of the knap. Think about asking a question through the gesture of the hands such as, "Why are you acting so aggressively?" or "Why are you trying to hurt me?"
- *Gesture #2*. Preparing for the body knap: before the strike take up a defensive gesture with both hands with one hand outstretched, the palm facing toward the aggressor. The other hand should be closer to the body with the palm facing the area on the body where the knap will be placed. For chest knaps or belly knaps this may work particularly well as a protective gesture.
- *Gesture #3*. Preparing for shared knaps: a defensive gesture can be used to great effect here as well. The knap hand of the receiver should be placed directly in the path of the hand that is performing the strike. Ideally upon contact for a shared knap involving hands, the hand should contact perpendicularly to each other for an optimum production of sound. The receiving hand could be gesturing as though it would have blocked the incoming attack. Rather the knap is made and the performer who receives the action reacts in a way that would register a successful hit.

We can see from the list of knaps that we can get a wide variety of location and sounds for each knap. It is up to the performers to be sensitive to the sound being made by the knap in relation to the body part being injured. You should make these choices as specific and varied as possible for each attack. A good rule of thumb for knaps is the same guidelines we can use for playing pain with vocalizations. The closer to the center of the body the attack lands typically the lower and more muted the sound is, such as a punch to the gut. As we move to the extremities, especially the head, the louder and more high pitched the knap can become. Think of a smack to the bones in the head or even the shin and what kind of sound one might expect to experience from such a blow.

As much as we should engage with a sense of realism for the quality of sound in each blow, we must never forget how the audience experiences that sound. As the great martial arts choreographer and film director Yuen Woo-Ping said, we must make the audience *feel* the blow. Of course we must pay attention to all of the other elements of precise physicality and clarity of storytelling through staging and character. However, if the sound is absent or incongruent to the experience of the viewing audience the effect of the violent moment is severely diminished. As a result we must augment the sound to intensify the experience for the audience. This can be achieved by being sensitive to three elements.

- *Pitch and volume.* Alter the level and quality of sound for each knap depending on the size of the venue. For small theaters, black boxes, and the like go for more intimate sounds with a few loud cracks for variety. For larger, proscenium houses, do vary the pitch of each knap depending on the location of the blow but lean towards making loud knaps that can carry to the back of the house for every shot.
- *Rhythm.* This should be underscored through the rhythm of the fight. Use the knaps to help create a rhythm that the audience can follow at times to create suspense for when the next hit will occur. Once you've established a rhythm you can then break that rhythm at key moments to surprise and startle the audience. As the great actor Jackie Chan said, "The audience don't know the rhythm is there until it's not there."
- *Vocal reaction.* This is the component of the soundscape in violence that is all too often disregarded. Either the vocalizations that are being made are too similar in duration and quality (a phenomenon affectionately called by choreographers as "grunts per move" or "GPM") or there is simply no sound being made at all. Quality vocal and breath reactions are so important in fact that they bear more in depth examination.

VOCALIZATIONS AND BREATH

Naturally, the knaps as varied as they may be should not be the only sounds heard in a stage fight. Use of breath and vocalizations is of more importance than we may realize in helping to create a complete story for a given fight. We further utilize the effects of sound made by the human body to elicit a desired and impulsive response from the audience. The techniques actors receive in vocal training can be put to good use when applied to stage violence.

There can be no vocalizations without breath. The respiratory system draws in air to the lungs and expels that air through the trachea and larynx where air encounters the vocal folds (or vocal cords) that oscillate in certain patterns to create sound and speech. But breathing affects much more than just the ability to make sound. The depth and pattern of breath can and does affect the degree to which the body is oxygenated, the rate at which the heart beats, and the quality of the musculature. Ultimately, breath is inexorably linked to the quality of bodily relaxation that is necessary to any performer.

There are two types of relaxation: passive and dynamic (Huxley, 1982: p.24). Passive relaxation is where the body has completely let go of any extraneous tension or energy and is in a state of complete repose. This type of relaxation can help restore one physically and psychologically from any trauma, however minor, that may have been experienced. However, passive relaxation is not enough. In order to move through the world, to achieve, to act (and act decisively), one must be able to function in a state of dynamic relaxation. In this state, the body and the mind work synergistically and economically, functioning in such a way that only the appropriate amount of effort needed to perform a given task, whether mental or physical, is used and nothing more. Dynamic relaxation is inexorably linked to tension. One cannot exist without the other. But what we must always remember is that the tension we allow into our bodies is *necessary* tension to perform the task at hand.

The act of breathing is just that, a physical act. It requires the use of structures of the body working in concert to produce a desired effect. The more relaxed the physical structures are the more output we can get out of this system. Most of us are not required in our daily lives to breathe beyond a certain limited range. In performance however, especially when performing moments of violence, the body is required to produce more breath than normal. There are two traps to performing scenes of violence when it comes to the breath: either there is too much breath or there is not enough.

Typically most problems arise from the latter. Performers cannot or will not engage with the imagined reality of the violent moment. They will shut down the respiratory system to such a degree that breathing will become very shallow or stop at points altogether. This is a terrible state to be in for obvious reasons. When there is no breath there is no life in the body nor between bodies. This makes for a terrible state for the actor to be in and an equally terrible thing for an audience to observe.

The former problem of too much breath can be equally as debilitating on the actor and the scene. When there is too much breathing (too rapid and too deep) this can actually increase the heart beat in such a way that fine motor skills begin to diminish. This would be detrimental to any scene requiring a complicated task, particularly one that involves choreography between performers. Additionally, too much breathing can actually distract an audience from other elements in the scene that may be more germane at the moment to further the story or the development of the characters.

Performers need to find opportunities to allow for natural breathing patterns to enter into a state of dynamic relaxation especially before performing a complicated task or entering into choreography. However, there are times when it is necessary for an actor to increase his or her breathing output in order to perform a task that requires more energy than before. Below are a few exercises that can help achieve these states of dynamic relaxation through breath in order to better perform moments of violence.

It should be noted that all of these techniques will be much more effective when the whole torso is filled with air. This means that not only the chest area is expanding upon inhalation but also the belly expands as the diaphragm lowers (also known as "diaphragmatic breathing"), the bottom of the ribcage swings out and to the side, and the back expands as well to get the full volume of breath into the lungs. For further techniques on developing lung capacity read Kristin Linklater's seminal work *Freeing the Natural Voice*.

TACTICAL BREATHING

This breathing technique has been employed by emergency responders, fire fighters, police, and military personnel to manage psychological and physical stress during and after events involving intense duress. This technique gained notoriety after being included in the book *On Combat: The Psychology and Physiology of Deadly Conflict in War and Peace* by David Grossman (2008). With practice it allows an individual to deescalate any extraneous tension in the body and actually helps lower the heart rate.

- Feeling the chest, belly, sides and back expand, breathe in fully through the nose on a count of 4.
- Hold the breath for a count of 4.
- Exhale through the mouth and nose on a count of 4.
- Hold the breath for a count of 4.
- Repeat at least 4 times or as many times as necessary to deescalate extraneous tension.

The counts for each part of the technique can increase up to 7 or even 10 depending on the physical capacity of a particular body. Most published sequences of tactical breathing involve holding the breath after both inhalation and exhalation. While this may be a useful element to the exercise in order to develop breath control, I would recommend that the breath *not* be held at any point in the technique, especially when being employed in a performance situation. The reason for this is two-fold. First, any interruption in the breath cycle may break the continuity and flow that a performer is in during a scene. Second, when a performer holds his or her breath that has a very particular effect on the audience. Oftentimes the audience will perceive there is a problem on stage when an actor holds his or her breath. This may take them out of the play if only for a moment. If the holding of the breath is something that is appropriate for the character at that moment then this part of the technique may prove useful. However, I would still recommend finding a way to move *through* the moment with the breath rather than holding it.

Instead of holding the breath, keep the air coming in during inhalation until you reach what feels like the absolute limit of your lung capacity. You may find that you have more capacity for the air than you thought were you to stop and hold it after the count of 4. Likewise, when exhaling, release all the air from the lungs to the point of pushing it out. After each inhale and exhale simply allow the respiratory system to naturally continue the cycle of breathing.

In order to increase the heart rate for those moments when a particular scene demands it (such as Macduff finding Macbeth at the end of the play) then we can use the sequence of tactical breathing as well by altering the duration of the inhalations and exhalations.

- Feeling the chest, belly, sides, and back expand, breathe in fully and audibly through the nose on a count of 1.
- Exhale fully through the mouth blowing through the lips and audibly through the nose on a count of 1.
- Repeat at least 4 times or as many as is necessary to increase heart rate.

Another alteration that is useful in increasing heart rate is to control each inhalation and exhalation further into 4 short, separated bursts. Each inhalation and exhalation should still be continuous but instead of one continuous breath it should now feel more percussive and staccato.

In addition, breathing out fully aids the performer in another way. Breathing out can actually increase the output during exertion for tasks requiring more power. It can also protect the body when receiving a blow. This is not only practically useful in a variety of ways. When receiving contact blows or making forceful bodily contact with another object one should exhale in order to take the blow. This allows the diaphragm to lift up and makes it less likely to spasm and seize as a result of a blow to the body (also known as "getting the wind knocked out of you"). Also, breathing upon exertion of an attack will give the audience the aural sensation that the performer is generating more power during the strike (which in fact is true if the breathing is done efficiently). This will add to the heightened quality of the violent moment through this use of breath. The theatrical quality will be even more heightened when vocals are added to the breath.

In order for the body to operate at peak efficiency the heart rate should be somewhere between 115 and 145 beats per minute. Anything above 145 beats per minute tends to diminish fine motor skills. The above breathing techniques can be used in conjunction with each other to either raise or lower the level of dynamic tension necessary for a given scene or situation. The more you practice these techniques the more easily you will be able to adjust your breath pattern.

Quite possibly the most important reason to breathe is this: it reminds whoever is watching you that we are all alive.

Of course, there cannot only be breath in a fight. For any violent moment to be complete there must be vocal sounds produced by the performers. The range of sound that can be produced by the human body is astonishing. Think of all of the vocalists from around the world and the kinds of different, nuanced sounds that can be created by the human body depending on training, style, culture, and environment. The sounds of violence should be as carefully scored and nuanced as any performed music piece. But of course most performers default to simply raising their volume and making horrible straining sounds with their voices.

And why not? Are not these realistic sounds that everyone has heard other human beings make in times of severe distress? Perhaps we even have had the experience ourselves of making such terrible screams in a moment when we felt most scared, most terrified, and most threatened. While the reality is that human beings can and do make such sounds in such moments of fear, this slavish attention to only one possible response to an incalculable number of particular violent moments will not serve the performer in the theatrical context. To have one type of vocal reaction (i.e. yelling and screaming) to every situation of violence in dramatic literature would be not only absurd, it would be downright boring. Would anyone be satisfied if Juliet reacted the same way to Romeo's death as Horatio did to the death of Hamlet? One of the great powers of the theatre is its ability to differentiate through nuance and exactitude how varied the human experience can be. Every production of a play is its own snowflake. No two stories are quite the same. It's the reason why people will still cram into the theater to see a production of *Hamlet* or *Romeo and Juliet* even though each play has been produced around the globe countless times over the last 400 years.

To explore the possibilities in making the sounds of violence we can begin by following a few simple rules born from our own experience. Think of the kind of sound you might make were you to be punched in the stomach. This would be like the sensation of "getting the wind knocked out of you." Would it be a high pitched, very loud sound or a low, muffled, guttural sound? Most people's experience, whether personal or having observed it in someone else, would probably say that the latter sound would be a more appropriate sound to expect to hear. What about if you stubbed your toe? Or got your thumb smacked by a hammer? Most likely the sound would be much louder and higher in pitch.

We can now develop a rudimentary guideline for producing appropriate violent sounds in performance that is rooted in physiological reality. The closer the trauma is to the center of the body, the lower in pitch the accompanying sound. The closer the trauma is to the extremities of the body, the higher in pitch the accompanying sound. This basic rule for sounds of course does not take into account volume, duration, or quality of sound. These other elements should be taken into account when finding the appropriate sound for a violent moment considering the size of the venue, the extent of the trauma, and the actor's interpretation of how the character would handle such pain.

CHAPTER 11

The Illusion of Violence

The theatre is not concerned with reality; it is only concerned with truth.

Jean-Paul Sartre

THE DISAPPEARING KNAP

If there is one technique that sets stage combat apart from any other discipline it is the use of the knap. The knap is an integral part of any given technique that involves a non-contact strike between performers. Practicing the knap to get just the right sound for a given moment and make it repeatable in performance takes time and care when considering the elements of volume and quality of sound for a strike. However, all of this good work in creating a full, vivid, and resonant moment of violence can disappear if the hands of the performer seem to do something unusual or unnatural. We must take care to make the act of knapping as fluid and seamless as possible. It is the vital part of the art that must never be seen. Knaps for the audience can never exist because they do not exist for the characters, only for the actor.

How do we achieve this? First start by simply clapping your hands together in a way that is relaxed and natural for you. Listen to the sound they make immediately. Think about the elements of volume and quality. Do you have a loud clap? A soft one? Is it a sharp sound? A dull one? Is it tinny or low in pitch? Do your hands sting after a few claps? How do you hold your hands when you clap? Are they angled? Are the palms slightly cupped or rigid? Do the hands come together directly in front of the torso or do they feel more comfortable slightly to the side?

After you have self-observed your clap, now begin to experiment with different ways in which you can clap your hands. Try striking the heel of your palm with your fingers while listening to the sound and feeling the sensation. Now try the back of one hand slapping the palm of the other. Try a clap that comes together and bounces back the way it came in. Now try one where the hands pass by each other and exchange positions. The possibilities are truly endless. Only by experimenting will you come to discover what way of knapping will be right for you. Knaps are like snowflakes, no two are quite the same. Even with a similar type of knap, say a clap knap for example, each time the knap is performed it will differ slightly in execution, feel, or sound. Finding the knaps that work for you is something only you can discover through individual practice and constant self-observation.

The clap knap is not the only knap available to a performer. The body knap is another useful and perhaps even more versatile knap technique available to the performer. The body knap is similar to the clap knap except instead of one hand striking the other, one hand strikes another part of the performer's body. The location of the knap could be anywhere. However, one will find that the most resonant, comfortable, and repeatable places on the body will be the regions with the most muscle mass. The pectorals, abdominals, latissimus dorsi, and outer gluteals typically make for some of the best locations. Additionally, these sounds can be made individually by a performer on his or her own body or they may be made between performers when one performer's hand strikes the hand or major muscle group of another performer. This will result in a shared knap. Whatever the technique of knap used experimentation is the key to finding the most appropriate knap for whatever is most appropriate for the violent interaction, most able to be heard, and most easily executed by the performer making the knap.

Making the knap seem not to exist can be helped most in the staging of the moment of violence. Typically the performer who is knapping should be positioned in such a way that he or she is facing away from the audience for the briefest of moments while the knap is happening. This should coincide with the moment of the strike. The standard staging for a strike in a proscenium theater where the audience is on one side of the room and the performers are on the other side is in the "offset" position. Here the performer receiving the blow (the receiver) and making the knap is facing completely upstage. The other performer who is performing the strike (the operator) should be facing downstage and upstage of the receiver. Also, the head of the operator should be visible over either the right or left shoulder of the receiver. Be certain not to end up in the "stacked" position as the body of the receiver who is downstage will eclipse the face of operator. This position allows the audience to see the character performing the aggressive action while using the masking of the receiver's body to hide the knap.

An immediate response to this kind of staging, especially from young directors, is that it breaks the cardinal rule of theatre that everyone who was ever in a play in grade school learned: never turn your back to the audience. This of course makes sense because when our parents came to see us in the school play they wanted to see our faces not our backs. Aside from placating parents everywhere with this rule, it serves a deeper conceptual purpose as well. The theatre, after all, is a place where things are supposed to be revealed. We go to see the "show." Naturally we want to see all things related to the telling of the story. Anything that is foreign or out of place takes the observer out of the narrative flow and the world of the play. Things must remain consistent throughout not necessarily between the outside world and the theatrical world but rather between the elements within the theatrical world that is created. This is part of the beauty and the madness of the theatre; anything is permissible as long as it is logically harmonious with the other elements in the play. Whatever rules those are should and must be followed. We can make up whatever rules we want as long as they tell the story in a clever, artfully satisfying way.

Let us assume that one of these rules is "hide the knap." If this is so, then how can we follow this guideline and still make sense of a particular violent moment considering we must hide a portion of the physical storytelling that we should ostensibly want to reveal?

As you may have noticed the pictures and the videos of techniques in later chapters are shown at two angles. The primary reason for this is to show the space that is necessary to avoid actually striking an actor while also giving a sense of how to optimally stage a technique to effectively convey that violent contact has been made (refer to Chapter 5 Audience Relationship (The Third Partner) for more on this). One perspective is meant to reveal the nuts and bolts of the technique for the actor, the other to illuminate the desired effect on an observing audience. Another reason for showing this staging is to start to understand where we may hide the knap (for more on the particular information on performing these refer to the section on knaps contained in Chapter 10). As is evident through the pictures, this upstage/downstage "offset" position where the person receiving the hit is typically downstage is maximal for hiding any knap. This staging allows the person who is being hit to easily manipulate his or her hands in front of the body to most easily create the desired sound. The hands can access each other, the major muscles groups of the pectorals, abdominals, and even the inner thigh quite easily in this position.

However, as has been mentioned before, remaining in this upstage/downstage offset position is dissatisfying for the audience because of previously ingrained notions of theatrical staging as well as the desire to see what is happening. In order to satisfy audience expectation, reveal reasons for the violent interaction, and obscure the knap we must not linger in the upstage/downstage offset position. Rather, we must move *through* these positions. This can be achieved though many means, not the least of which is clever staging. The blocking of a scene leading up to a violent moment must not be taken from simply the line before the hit. The genesis of the desire to hit typically starts growing many scenes before. Going back at least half a page or even a full page in the script is necessary to investigate not only how the emotional life is beginning to change between the characters but also how the physical interaction alters leading up to the strike. The pattern of changing body postures in each character should lead naturally to the moment of violence.

This is easy to say and much more difficult to do. Too often I have seen an excellent scene full of life and spontaneity suddenly become stolid and wooden without warning. The reason would invariably be that the actors were shedding the interactions of the characters and transitioning into "safe-stage-combat-technique-mode." Movement becomes blocking; acting becomes technique. This is also typically accompanied by a slight ritardando in the tempo of the scene. The audience can see and feel the hit coming from a mile away. Ideally we should want the hit to happen suddenly and spontaneously without warning. If it is a surprise for the character it should be a surprise for the audience as well. If the actors and director think about the staging of the hit being the end point, the pinnacle that they want to reach for a certain moment, then they can more easily start to investigate how to get there naturally and logically using the moments that lead up to it.

A simple trick to use here in staging is to throw in a push or grab right before the hit. This allows the actors to still face each other in profile and then use movement to get themselves into the upstage/downstage offset position to perform the hit. This does not necessarily mean that the performers are actually moving while the hit is being performed. While this is a possible choice, performing non-contact strikes while in motion may muddy the clarity of the strike and is also much more difficult to perform in terms of precision and safety than a strike that happens with the performers stationary. Keeping the feet stable and grounded during the moment of the strike will help promote maximum precision of the technique and also allow more time to find the necessary spacing to keep the actors from injuring each other. In this position the knap can be done without being in clear view of the audience.

It is at this moment that the knap comes into its own. The sound should be clear and precise. The audience should respond not only to the violent motion but the sharp, staccato sound being produced as well. The hands should remain relaxed throughout and completely gestural before and after the strike. It is only at the moment of the actual knap that these hands are performing a technique. This should only take a fraction of a second. Throughout the rest of the violent moment, the hands of the receiver must be doing something as exact as the hands of the operator.

The operator has so many things on which to focus: the target of the strike, the shape of the hand performing the violence, the muscular tension necessary to perform the action. There is typically so much emphasis placed on performing the action of the technique we can lose the specificity of what is involved in receiving the action. This is not too surprising since people, especially performers, can be obsessed with performing an action and performing it as well as possible. But we forget that in this particular instance this interaction is a shared moment. The reaction is necessary to complement the action. We can't have one without the other. If one is clearly defined but the other is not then the system as a whole breaks down. The continuation of the story being told is as much if not more so about the results of what changes after violence has been done as it is about the why and how one person chooses to hurt another human being. Attention to the physical life of the person reacting is necessary to aid in the continuation of the story.

In order to move through the moment and not have the performers remain in a static but a dynamic upstage/downstage offset position they need to open up and reveal the picture. This is easily done by the performer receiving the hit moving his or her body in the direction of the force of the hit. Naturally the part of the body that has been targeted (most likely the head) moves in the direction of the strike. Once that part of the body moves first, the rest of the body naturally follows. Be mindful of how far the head moves in relation to the strike. The neck is a very flexible but also delicate instrument. Repeated sudden movements with the head and neck can lead to pain and discomfort in a very short period of time. Always make sure that the head does not turn past 45 degrees from neutral (looking straight ahead).

Once the head reaches this maximum angle of 45 degrees from looking straight ahead one should relax the neck muscles and allow the head to return to neutral. Also, the shoulders of the body can turn in the direction that the head is moving to relieve any strain on the neck. What ends up happening is a spiraling action down the spine that starts and ends in the neutral position. What should be different is the distance between the performers. The feet obviously have a role in this as they move in such a way as to keep the performer balanced through the reaction while giving the illusion of being off-balance. The distance or measure between the performers should have gone from a closed position in order to hide the knap and the space for the strike to an open position where they can carry on the rest of the scene. This increased distance also helps communicate to the audience the transference of force that is very important in creating the illusion of violence.

Now of course one can overdo it with reactions. All too often an actor receives a punch and it sends him or her halfway across the stage. Overreactions break the illusion of violence. Likewise, under-reacting or under-performing a strike drains the moment of any consequence. The actors must always walk the line between being faithful to the reality of the violence while animating the action in such a way as to make it crystal clear to an observing audience exactly what the action was and the effect of how it was received.

Naturally, a strike that is thrown with great force (such as a 9 on a scale of 1–10) should be paired with a reaction of equal magnitude. Likewise, a strike that has less force behind it (say at a value of 3) should be paired with a reaction that moves the receiver in a less forceful manner. Even if the hit is very light for whatever the reason there still must be a reaction! If there is a scene with a small woman who weighs 95 pounds with a large man who weighs 225 pounds and the woman must slap the man in the face or punch him in the gut, the man must still react both physically and emotionally in some way. There must always be a reaction and a consequence to any action of violence so that the relationship between the two characters then changes. In reality perhaps the man would not budge at all because the force generated from the woman wouldn't be sufficient to do so. However, if there is no reaction there is diminished readability of the interaction to the audience. It is not enough for the performers to have it in their minds how they imagine the interaction is supposed to be. They must *show* it to the audience.

The relationship between the action and the reaction is perhaps the most vital aspect of the illusion of violence. The magnitude of the reaction must be commensurate to the magnitude of the action. Whenever there is a discrepancy between the values each performer gives to a particular strike the effect invariably becomes comical. Now if this is the intent of the interaction, say for slapstick comedy, then that is something the actors can certainly play. But for the bulk of violent interactions shown in theatre and film, particularly dramatic work, any sense of humor during the action of the strike and reaction to it undercuts the gravitas of the moment.

The illusion of violence is not just about the austerity or severity of a situation gone awry. It is also about wonder. This wonder should occur on two fronts. The first front should be the technical wonder of, "How did they do that? Did she really hit him?" In the back of their minds, the audience knows it's all a sham. Those people on stage or on screen aren't really who they claim to be, nor is any of this really happening in such a way that affects the rest of the world. It is a closed system. But it is a system in which the audience is now complicit. In the moment of witnessing the violence the audience should never think, "I know how they did that." In this case the man behind the curtain is seen and the illusion is broken. The skill involved in executing the technique must be so precise in terms of specificity of the target attacked, proper angle to show the action of the violence and yet hide the tricks we use to keep the actors safe, and matched magnitude of force between action and reaction that the audience is compelled to believe what happened on stage was absolutely true in that moment.

The second front should be the wonder of, "How could one human being do that to another human being?" This does not mean that the audience should not know the reason for the violence. There should always be a reason for the violence depicted in theatre and film regardless of whether we as performers or the audience think that the reason for violence is a justifiable one. It could be completely unjustified, but we could still clearly see the reason why a character punches, slaps, kicks, or gouges the eyes out of another character. We enact violence in this way to examine it fully. We wonder at it to attempt to understand the human capacity for violence. If a moment of violence is enacted with sincerity of intent, skill of technique, and mindfulness of consequence then in that moment the audience should believe, even if only for a fraction of a second, that those performers are characters doing harm to one another.

CHAPTER 12

Non-contact
Violence

It takes great effort to make something look effortless.

Degas

On the set of a short film two hockey players were about to throw down and have a fist fight against the boards. I had rehearsed the fight with both actors a week before. They were both professional actors, able-bodied, and very good skaters. During one take, one actor threw an uppercut to the other actor, sending the second actor sprawling onto the ice. At that moment the crew let out a gasp. Suddenly the director called, "Cut!" after which she immediately called to the actor on the ice "Are you all right?" The actor got up without a problem and said, "Yeah, why?"

"We thought you were hurt."
"No, I'm fine."
"It looked so real."
"That's because it's my job. It's supposed to look real."

Non-contact violence when done properly and with skill and commitment to the action can seem just as real to an observer as the actual thing. On some occasions, using non-contact violence can actually be even more useful particularly when the performers are not yet comfortable enough in their training and experience to actually lay hands upon one another. Non-contact violence relies on all the same criteria that contact violence does such as precision of target, expressive physicality connected to intent, and commensurate magnitude of reaction to the action. However, the one added element of non-contact violence that makes it an even more demanding part of the craft is its reliance on the proper angle of presentation. Many of these concepts for proper use of non-contact violence have been mentioned in Chapter 11 ("The Illusion of Violence"). All of the topics covered in each chapter will inform each other so be sure to be familiar with each one to get a full picture.

There is one inviolable rule when it comes to non-contact strikes during dramatic violent interactions. The audience can under no circumstances whatsoever see the space between performers during the action of the strike. Either the distance between the performers must be reduced or the angle of presentation of the move must be set so that the space disappears.

Let us remind ourselves that the space between performers exists to begin with because on some strikes the target simply cannot be struck, particularly the head and face for what I hope are obvious reasons (actors tend to like to keep concussed heads and bloody faces to a minimum). So for most of our discussion of non-contact moves the target will most likely be the head. There are other times when non-contact strikes can be applied to other body parts such as the stomach. However, the majority use for non-contact hits remains the noggin.

Hiding the space from the audience becomes a more difficult sensibility for an actor to cultivate than it may originally seem. When making a swing at the receiver the operator of the action usually sees the hand cross the plane of the face in such a way that the action reads visually as a hit to both actors. However, to an observing audience the angle of perception is most likely totally different than that of the performers. As a result the actors have to have a clear idea of what the audience is seeing during the moment of performing the violent action. For actors who place a premium on being "in the moment" this can present somewhat of a problem since having an awareness outside of the immediate interaction may prove distracting to maintaining focus. However, in order for this moment to be fully realized the actor must expand his or her awareness to include the audience. The audience then becomes a partner in the work. They become another receiver of the action. If the violent action is done with skill and with this in mind then some audience members may react physically and psychologically in a manner similar to the character who is the target of the violence on stage. Some audience members may also react in a way that is similar to the perpetrator of the violence. If the actors are doing their job and the story is clear then this act of transference should be happening constantly throughout the play. The audience will feel if only for a moment the force of the blow and become involuntarily complicit in the violence.

How can actors develop this sensibility for closing off the space for non-contact violent moves? The following are some strategies for dealing with such moments:

- *Put the target directly between you and the audience.* This is the easiest and most effective way to make sure a hit reads. If the performer who needs to get hit is between you and the audience (particularly downstage) then the chances that the hit will read as such become considerably greater. By extension, if it is impossible to put your whole body on the other side of the target from the audience then at least the body part doing the strike (hand, fist, foot, etc.) must be on the other side of the target from the viewing audience.
- *Put your body between the target and the audience.* This technique also works but is slightly less effective. Here the audience may see less of the actual moment of the hit since the operator of the move would be facing upstage. While it is still possible to get a hit to read in this way, this technique has more of a chance when the body of one actor

eclipses the body of the other actor. As a result selling the hit relies more on a clear reaction by the actor getting hit. By extension, the actor can also place the body part doing the strike between the target and the viewing audience. This may open up the picture to actually see the moment of the hit. However, a trade-off is that it then makes it even more difficult for the receiver to make a knap that won't be immediately visible to the audience. This orientation is recommended to work best with performers who are very adept at knapping.

- *Move the entire body through the course of the strike.* This technique employs body camouflage as a means to divert attention from any possible space between performers and knaps. The idea behind this is that the audience will be more likely to look at the large body moving through space than what the smaller hands are doing. This technique, while useful, requires even more training and sensitivity since multiple limbs are moving simultaneously throughout the technique.

No matter what technique you choose to employ the inviolable directive remains – *do not let the audience see the space.* If the audience sees the space and the actors react as though there was a hit then the illusion of violence in that moment and of the whole piece is lost. The performers cease to be viewed as something the audience believes to be true and become humans play-acting as though they were small children.

One of the drawbacks to non-contact striking techniques is that there is something missing that is present in contact techniques. During contact moves when a solid attacking object meets another solid target object there is a momentary interruption in the path of the attacking object. For example, when a fist contacts the abdominal muscles there is a slight interruption in the bodies of both operator and receiver. Both bodies *pulse* for a moment before completing the action and reaction. This pulse is a small but important element to add to non-contact techniques to simulate the exact moment of contact. There are a variety of ways to introduce this pulse into a given technique. A good way to initiate the pulse at the point of perceived contact is to give the hand or fist a little flick or shake. On a non-contact slap, for example, the performer may visualize flicking water off of the fingertips to achieve the pulse. A former student, when performing non-contact slaps and punches, used to say she would "throw the fire" in her partner's face. Apart from the obvious attachment to Aristotelian elemental images, there could be a variety of other images or sensations that could be of use. Whatever the method, add the pulse to non-contact moves to give them an added level of authenticity.

Reactions to non-contact moves must be commensurate to the magnitude and speed of the action as always. Not only this, but the angle of the reaction, must be commensurate to the angle of the attack. If a punch is travelling horizontally to the receiver's right, then the head had better move in that direction as well. If another punch starts from above and to the left of the receiver and follows a track down and to the right then the head should move down and to the right. In short, the performer receiving the hit should look and follow the path of the attacking object to match its trajectory.

Another challenge to non-contact moves is that unlike moves involving contact the receiver must react at the right time for the hit to be believable. React too early and the move could be read as a miss. React too late and the jig is up; it will look as though the actors are not in the same scene at all. For any strike to the head the optimal time to react is when the attacking object is right in front of the eyes. The path of the strike may follow a straight line as though it passed through the head or the strike may be pulled back as though it "bounced" off of the head. In either case the reaction should be timed to happen in the middle of the path of the violent movement.

NECK EXERCISES

The following are a few simple neck mobility exercises when preparing for a session that will focus particularly on non-contact violence involving head reactions. These are a series of isometric exercises to engage the musculature of the neck in preparation for head reactions. Isometrics are a type of strength training performed in static rather than dynamic range of motion positions in which joint angle and muscle length do not change during contraction (https://en.wikipedia.org/wiki/Isometric_exercise). Personally, I wish that I had learned these earlier in my career as I imagine they would have allowed for supported freedom and range of motion through my reactions. However, I did not learn these until having worked with a physical therapist when I was experiencing some neck discomfort. Use your best judgement in the force applied to these following exercises. You will find that they will increase the range of motion possible in articulating the neck. Just be certain that you never exceed your own natural range of motion in the cervical spine.

For the first exercise simply turn the head to look easily to the right. Do not strain to look over the right shoulder nor should you turn the shoulders or waist to look in this direction. After you notice how far you can naturally turn your head to the right return to the neutral position looking straight forward. Now place the palm of the right hand against the right temple. Without moving the head out of the neutral position, push against the head with the right palm while attempting to turn the head to the right just as you did the moment before. Remember, since this is an isometric exercise the head will actually not move from the neutral position of looking forward. You should feel the muscles of the neck engage, especially along the right side. Think long in the neck as you send your energy both into the resisting palm and up towards the sky. Do this for at least a count of 10 increasing the isometric force gradually along the way. When you release the force relax for a moment and then take the same easy look to the right. After this exercise most people find that the range of motion looking in the same direction has increased and can be performed with less effort. Bring the head back to neutral and take an easy look to the left. Notice the natural range of motion first. Then repeat the isometric detailed above with the left palm against the left temple increasing the force through a count of 10. Finally, look once again to the left to see how much extra range of motion is attained through turning the head.

The isometric exercises can be performed with head tilts as well. You may utilize the same sequence of naturally performing the action first to notice the natural range of motion; then using the palm of the hand on the same side the action is performed to provide the isometric pressure. I would recommend doing these exercises in at least four directions of the head tilt: left, right, forward, and back. Please note that tilting the head without isometric resistance should not be done in such a way that crunches the muscles or joints, especially when moving the head backwards. When moving in any of these directions think up and out, letting the weight of the head dictate the amount of extension with no additional force. Particularly when tilting the head to the rear imagine you are about to hold on to a grapefruit between your occiput (the bottom ridge portion of the back of the skull) and the upper part of the back and shoulder blade. Do not move the head and neck all the way back as though it were the top of a Pez dispenser. This action, even when done slowly, invariably leads to overextension of neck muscles and major compression of the discs between the cervical vertebrae. If time permits, I would recommend performing these isometrics in an additional four directions: forward right, forward left, back left, and back right with the same directions and caveats as before. These directions are also useful to prepare for different angles of non-contact punches or slaps to the head.

Having an expressive body from head to toe can be of great use to the conscientious performer. An animated torso and spine should propel the movement out through the limbs of the body during any given action and reaction. Traditionally when thinking about the limbs of the human body most people think of four in total – two arms and two legs. However, if a limb is an extension of the torso then we actually have six limbs altogether: two arms, two legs, the head and the tail. Granted the head and tail are part of the spine but why shouldn't they be as expressive as any other limb? All of the limbs should be expressive and engage throughout the fight, not just the limbs performing or receiving the action.

12.1

These should include not only the arms that punch and kick but also the hips (or tail) that generate power and direction of action and the head that sees and reacts to those actions.

Animating all of these limbs and making them active in every movement leads to a greater connection between performers and a greater expressivity of action for any observer to see. Once I met a librarian in the arts library at a school I was visiting who was helping me look for a book. Through the course of our conversation she asked me what I did and I told her my specialty. Her eyes widened and she started to gush about how she loved every sort of action movie. She particularly loved Bruce Lee and Jackie Chan. She spoke of specific scenes with such relish and excitement. She then mentioned how she always looked forward to seeing theatre shows that have stage combat. In the moment immediately following she paused. As her brows knitted together she looked at me and said, "Why does stage combat always look so bad?" My heart sank but I knew what she meant. If there is one culprit that turns an enthusiastic audience member who yearns to see exciting violence as part of a theatrical production into a bored theatre-goer it is this; productions treat the violent moments in a play as a placeholder that must be endured and trudged through in order to get to the other more "important" parts of the play. There is a lower quotient of expressivity not only physically but also in the context of propelling the story forward to something new. Usually this is because nobody in the production knows how to craft that moment with skill and care. Also, no one takes into account what the audience sees. Any moment of violence is an opportunity to excite the audience, to make them invest more deeply in the story and the characters because something is happening that is terrible, unusual, and changes the course of events from that moment forward. This is not a moment for artists to shrink from. It is a moment for artists to embrace! A basic understanding of how to stage non-contact violence is a step in the right direction. If every actor and director would learn and perfect three non-contact striking techniques then 80% of the violent moments that are written into plays could be covered without anxiety.

CHAPTER 13

Contact Violence

INITIATING CONTACT

"So Rob, why do we have a fight call?"

The words would have floated past me had Shira not said my name. It is the Wednesday night of tech week and we open on Saturday. We had been rehearsing Qui Nguyen's "She Kills Monsters" for Company One in Boston for nearly two months and everyone from the cast to the design team to the administrative staff had put in loads of man-hours just to get the show into a recognizable form. There were so many elements to blend: weapons, props, lighting in a strange semi-thrust space, puppets of all shapes and sizes, costumes for succubi, devils, and elves, big cheerleader dance numbers, and of course, the fights. The blending of all these elements was due to the brilliant collaborating skills of everyone involved but particularly the orchestration of the director, Shira. But like all complicated endeavors it took a lot of coordinating, massaging, and work. At this hour of the night after a 10 out of 12, sitting through a production meeting with a small army of designers was the last thing I, or presumably anyone else, wanted to be doing. I had glazed over in a way that I had heard monks used to when staying up for days, the world just passing before them as a separate entity not really connected to anything human. Shira's questions snapped me back.

"There are 7 full on fights in this show. The fight call will be crazy long. Do we have to do a fight call? Why do we need it?"

It took me a while before I realized everyone had shut up to listen to my reply. The first three sentences that came out of my mouth didn't make any comprehensible sense. I would like to think the gobbledygook was an effort to not come back with the parental reply of, "Because that's how it's always been done." Finally, the most essential thing I could manage at that hour was, "It's their warm-up." Warm-ups, it seems, is something that just about everyone who has trained for or worked in theatre can understand. The actors need their warm-up time and this is part of it.

Later on my simple response hadn't satisfied me. Why do they need to warm up? They have been doing this for two months. Can't they remember their movements like they remember their lines? Why this time to review and check in? I thought about how much physical and vocal warming up I do when I am about to perform (not nearly enough as my voice teacher in graduate school Ellen O'Brien would like, I reckon) and it occurred to me how necessary it is to prime the instrument of the human body before any kind of contact is made. I was painting with broad strokes in my mind and thought how this could be true of any kind of contact: emotional, psychological, and physical. It takes time, space, and practice for a human to open up and be receptive to another person. That's one of the reasons ensemble training works so well. The players have a history of trust and connection with each other that they can rely on to deepen and expand the work of creating relationships and story on stage. They don't have to think about or worry about the problems associated with negotiating the moment of initial contact.

As intelligent as the body is it can sometimes forget what it is capable of when presented with what it perceives as a threat to its own safety. It doesn't forget easily, but when it comes to moments of highly engaged physicality, especially that which involves the probability or necessity of impact, the body can be jarred in such a way to interrupting the flow of action. This is why the fight call is necessary. It prepares the body for the impact to come. All scenes on stage involve impact. The degree to which that impact happens varies greatly, but people can recognize good theatre when they see it. And what they see is impact. The impact of a man seeing his future wife for the first time, the impact of someone leaving a lover, the impact of a broken expectation, the impact of a mother losing her child, the impact of a son dealing with the death of his father. Perhaps the simplest form of this impact is when one human being feels compelled to physically lay hands on another in order to express what has heretofore been inexpressible because all other modes of communication have failed. When we know it's coming we tense all the muscles in our body and brace for impact. If we believe what most of our acting teachers have told us that extraneous tension is the enemy of an expressive body, then we must find a way to prepare for receiving such contact in a way that affects us and yet we go on and grow and learn from the contact instead of denying it.

We fight call. We train. We prepare. As Hamlet says, "The readiness is all." The body will forget. It will flinch. It will tense. It will protect itself. Impact probes weakness, probes vulnerability. On stage we wish to reveal things. We can wear the armor but we must reveal the chinks. We must allow ourselves to receive the blow so we can feel its effect.

CONTACT PUNCHES TO LARGE MUSCLE GROUPS

With regard particularly to contact punches to major muscle groups (to the abdominals, latissimus dorsi, pectoralis major, rhomboids, hamstring, etc.), I prefer having more emphasis on the action moving to the target than away. The idea of "pulling the punch" or "reverse energy" is a well-intentioned one in terms of attempting to protect the receiver of the punch. However, what ends up happening is that the operator puts more emphasis, effort, and speed to that part of the movement that travels away from the target. This ends up giving the impression to an observer that the operator didn't mean to punch the receiver. The perceived intent of the aggressive action appears to end up becoming more of an apology on the character's part or, technically speaking, a way for the actor performing the punch to actively demonstrate how safe he or she is keeping the receiver.

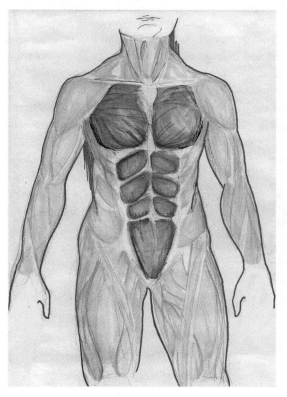

13.1

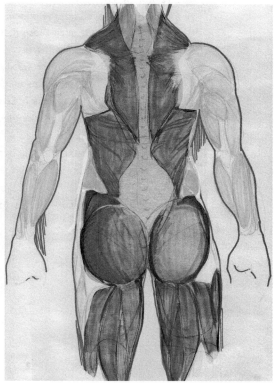

13.2

Barring headshots (which for our purposes should never be attempted for reasons made only too obvious by increased national awareness of the serious health risks posed by repeated trauma to the brain through collisions in contact sports such as American football), body shots to major muscle groups should be something that any actor with training should be able to explore in rehearsal and perform in a production either on the giving or receiving end. The roadblocks to performing these for most actors I find are mostly psychological rather than physical. Typically, and perhaps surprisingly, most of the time it is the actor doing the punching who is most distressed by this technique for fear of hurting the fellow actor. If a cast has been assembled and the actors haven't had any previous professional or social interaction with each other this can exacerbate the situation because one actor is being asked to punch another actor whom he or she may have just met. Alternatively, if the two actors have been working together in an ensemble for some time they may be friends and wouldn't dream of injuring each other. (Some ensembles, depending on the day or hour of the day, want to genuinely throttle each other. This situation of course presents its own dangers. For a review of safety concepts turn to Chapter 3 Seeking Safety). Of course, there is concern for the person receiving the punch. Perhaps the actor has never been on the receiving end of a violent action. Or even more delicate of a situation, perhaps the actor had experienced a violent trauma earlier in his or her life and this aggressive action brings up disconcerting memories and feelings of the transgression. Whatever the case, the most important aspect of initiating contact with a fellow actor is to *talk about it.* I cannot stress how important this is and how easily it is to gloss over. At the beginning it's necessary to be very prescriptive about the location of the punch, the intended force behind it, and to make sure the actor who is receiving the punch is indeed ready to receive it.

A performer should know how to take a hit – or a fall for that matter. This knowledge from training and experience keeps the performer safe on his or her own terms. Having conceptual and physical knowledge of what the body (and his or her body in particular) is capable of handling is invaluable for artistic expression and professional longevity.

THE FLOATING PALM/THE FLOATING FIST

Start by using a relaxed hand to contact major muscle groups on a partner. Begin slowly and concentrate on being sensitive to quality of touch and sound produced from the contact. When both partners have taken a turn priming each others' bodies with their palms then use light punches against a major muscle group to develop accuracy and sensitivity. This should start at a slow pace agreed upon by both players until accuracy develops. As skill and accuracy increase move to other major muscle groups on the body. Keep the contact light and to the target that you are striking rather than extending or pushing through it. Feel free to experiment with different parts of the entire body. However, note that any strike to joints, genitals, the throat, eyes, ears, or the nose are typically avoided altogether since they are extremely sensitive and delicate areas of bodily function and should be protected at all times. As you become more comfortable with your partner and the quality of contact, experiment with changing the pace of the game or the level of contact, either increasing or decreasing the tempo or force of each strike. As the striker is investigating where appropriate targets are for not injuring the receiver, the receiver is experimenting with making playable reactions depending on the speed, force, and location of the strike. These reactions should be tailored to only the energy that is being received by the striker. Resist the temptation to over-emphasize a reaction to a very light punch or not move and "take" a strike from someone simply because you know you can. See how fluidly you can move from one move to the next. Variations include strikes with the feet (sole, instep, or top of the foot [Figures 13.3–13.5]), the knees (top of the thigh or quadricep), and elbows (tricep).

13.3   **13.4**   **13.5**

The location of the strike is important while targeting large muscle groups in order for the receiver to effectively disperse the energy of the hit. The operator of the action can also aid in reducing the impact by making the strike with a relaxed fist. The first is not tightly packed (Figure 13.6) but rather has some space between the pads of the fingertips and the palms (Figure 13.7). This space would be akin to holding a few straws or pencils in the grip of the fist. This gives the hand the appearance of having the structure of a fist without having the same penetrating power as if the fist were tightly held.

13.6   **13.7**

Additionally, the contacting surface of the fist should be as flat as possible. The suggested strikes mentioned previously of the foot, knees, and elbows are all actually delivered with the flat structures that connect to those points. To make a strike with the point of the knee or elbow can be devastating to both operator and receiver alike. All of the force generated is contained in that one point of contact and can lead to penetrating damage even if it meets a large muscle group. That is why the sole, instep, or top of the foot are preferable striking surfaces than the ball, heel, or outside edge of the foot. For similar reasons the triceps should be used on an elbow strike as the quadriceps should be used on a knee strike. Even the hand when made into the fist can be rotated in 4 ways to expose a flat surface to meet the area of impact. The back, bottom, and front of the fist all have flat surfaces where the contact becomes more comfortable. The bottom of the fist has a smaller surface area than the other three orientations of the fist and therefore does have more chance of containing penetrating force. However, it is still an available option if the magnitude of the force is monitored. If the fist is rotated in such a way that the knuckles are the first points of contact then any force will be concentrated into those points leading to penetrating pressure and possible damage during the strike.

Having a flat surface while making a strike is of particular importance when exploring one of the most widely misunderstood techniques in all of theatrical violence: the contact slap. If any one technique causes the most anxiety among performers, directors, stage managers, or even the light board operator, it's this one. The anxiety is well founded. Human contact anywhere above the neck is intimate. When there is an increase in the force of that contact the body immediately shifts to a defensive mode to protect the vital functions located in the head such as seeing, breathing, hearing, smelling, and of course thinking. It is possible with time, patience, practice, and trust that the contact slap can be a seamless part of the scene. But if the technique is insisted upon without the proper time and careful preparation it can grind production to a halt.

I was asked to come in to stage a slap for a mainstage production of a large regional house. The company manager had said to me that it was "just a slap." After reading through the play I came in about halfway through the rehearsal process to see what kind of staging would be involved. However, when I arrived no definite staging had been set. While it was possible to choreograph the violent action without previous staging, it was more difficult to determine an organic cause leading up to the slap. Additionally the director said, "I need it to be real. None of this stagey, non-contact stuff. I know there's a way to make contact slap that's safe and that's what I want." The nature of this request may have been a good way to start off the conversation in week one of rehearsal but with only an hour to devote to the scene staging the director didn't realize that he was asking for more than the time permitted. But the actors seemed game so I asked them how comfortable they felt with exploring the contact slap. They all nodded their heads and seemed ready to try it out. Then the actor who was supposed to get slapped said, "Of course I'll do whatever is good for the scene. I just want you to know that I have nerve damage in my left cheek so that can't be hit." I turned to the other actor doing the slapping. "How comfortable are you slapping her with your left hand." His response was one like most right-handed people of the world. "I haven't even looked at my left hand in years." We experimented with his left hand doing the slap. We even tried other violent actions involving contact other than the slap. After the hour, everyone was frustrated. We were attempting to fit a square peg on the contact slap in the round hole of actor who did not have the time nor physical skills to do the particular technique the director insisted upon. There just wasn't the time to make the contact techniques precise enough that they looked organic to the scene. Eventually after much negotiating and questioning the production ended up with a standard, proscenium non-contact slap with a clap knap. A bit stagey? Perhaps. But it worked consistently every night in performance.

Had the director identified his wishes for a contact slap at the first rehearsal then it gives the actors a fighting chance to actually own the technique. The process takes time and practice every day. This prepares the area being hit for the contact gradually. When there is a gradual build-up of increased contact the body is better prepared to receive the blow. Below is a process of preparing for a contact slap between two actors.

The Contact Slap

- The actor doing the slapping should strike his or her own face first. That's right. The person doing the slapping hits himself or herself first. This gives the operator of the action a direct experience of how the hand will connect with the face.
- The person receiving the slap strikes his or her own cheek, the cheek to be hit in performance. As the receiver strikes his or her own cheek repeatedly the operator of the action looks to see the location and force of the slap. The operator also listens to the quality of the sound being made upon contact. This gives the operator information about how vigorously the receiver is comfortable being slapped. It also primes the cheek for continued contact for the rest of rehearsal.
- The receiver takes hold of the slapping hand of the operator and places that hand in the spot on the cheek where the receiver would like to be struck. This should ideally be on the meat of the cheek where the fingers of the operator are not intruding upon the ears, nose, mouth, or eyes (Figure 13.8).

13.8

- From this position the operator tries to emulate the quality and force of the slap the receiver was doing to himself or herself earlier in the rehearsal process. The slap of the operator should not travel too far away from the cheek. Rather the hand should try to recreate the exact same quality and sound of the original slap by the receiver with as little distance to travel as possible.
- Gradually the hand can be drawn farther away from the target cheek. However, the force and quality of the contact should remain as close to the original as possible. This develops the operator's sensitivity to maintain the amount of force transferred to the receiver despite increasing the distance between the hand and the cheek.

- The path of the slapping hand should track from a relaxed position where it can contact the cheek on a 90-degree angle (Figure 13.9). The hand should not swing up from the hip as the upward diagonal trajectory may hit the ears or eyes while swinging up.

13.9

- Once contact is made special care should be taken to make sure that the force of the strike does not push through the head. Upon contact, the hand should have the quality of slightly rebounding off of the cheek. Note that this rebound is not like a trampoline. The rebound is only a fraction of an inch in order to ensure that the force of the strike only travels to the target rather than through it (Figure 13.10).

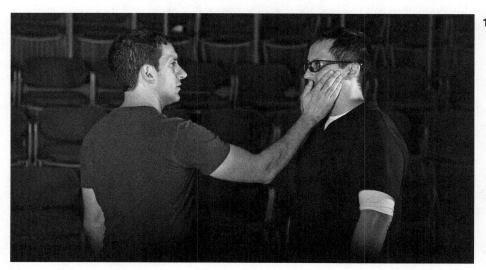

13.10

- Once the rebound occurs, the hand should relax and track down on the same line as that of the receiver's jaw line (Figure 13.11).

13.11

- After each strike, the receiver of the slap should verbally communicate with the operator if the force of the slap was too hard, too soft, or just right. This should happen after every slap. The operator should adjust each slap according to the feedback of the receiver.
- The most important element to this technique is the quality of sound. If there is not a good "crack" to the slap then there is not much reason to include it in the scene. Both partners therefore should strive to get the best quality of sound from the contact slap as comfortably as possible.

Once all of these steps have been followed for the interaction of the slap then the roles are reversed. The receiver of the action then goes through all the steps of slapping the operator of the action even though this may never happen in performance. Why do this? It is a human response to have particular feelings about the person who is striking us repeatedly. No matter how professional we may profess to be, how well we know the person doing the strike or how agreeable we say we may be with being hit repeatedly, there will always be some awkward sentiments that arise between partners when one partner is hitting the other on an exclusive basis. By sharing the process in both directions during rehearsal the playing field is leveled. This reversal allows both partners to participate fully in the violent moment to understand the physical reality of both side on the equation.

The above process can actually be used for *any* staged moment of contact violence for striking (punch, kick, elbow, knee) no matter what the target provided that target is to a major muscle group. The main caveat here is that in rehearsal and performance, the strike goes *to* the target and not *through* the target. This is a wildly different concept from martial arts or pugilism where strikes travel through the intended target to cause maximum damage. The only effect the receiver of a stage combat contact strike should feel is perhaps a slight sting to the skin of the target being attacked. Everything else necessary to the reaction should be animated in a way that is commensurate with the action and intent of the attack.

Taken for Granted (Skills Every Actor is Expected to Know)

We are what we repeatedly do. Excellence then is not
an act, but a habit.

Aristotle

"I'm going to ask you for something and feel free to say no if you're not comfortable with it but . . . can you fall backwards?" The director of the commercial I was auditioning for asked me this intently with an inflection that suggested he had requested the impossible. I had performed two falls for him, the casting director, and the producer on the other side of the table already, both landing on the blue mat face first. The first time I fell I made such a loud noise hitting the mat that the casting director jumped a bit from her chair. Falls landing face first are always a bit more strenuous than falls on the back since the reverb from hitting the ground causes the spine to curve away from the floor. Since the spine naturally curves towards the anterior or front of the human body this makes falling backwards preferable especially when performing the fall repeatedly. I know this. The director apparently does not.

I furrowed my brow and returned the director's gaze and slowly nodded my head. I took three paces onto the blue mat again, kicked my feet up going horizontal a few feet above the ground, and landed flat on the mat with a smack. I got up as if nothing had happened. The director came over and shook my hand. I booked the job on the spot and with it my SAG card.

I was lucky that the part required a skill that I had been practicing for years. All of the martial arts I had taken had helped me develop a sense of how to go to the floor. However, it was not until I had taken stage combat in graduate school that I truly discovered how to go to the floor consistently without injuring myself while making maximum sound. This is a very specific skill set that is particular to performers. The techniques that follow are staples of the acting trade. They might not always be the ones that land you the job. But they will certainly be the ones that directors, producers, and other trained actors will expect you to be familiar with when doing professional work.

GOING TO THE GROUND

Going from a standing position to a position on the floor is one indispensable skill for an actor to possess. Every actor should be able to do a controlled fall from standing to the ground in either the supine (face up) or prone (face down) position in a variety of situations, whether from a push, a punch, a gunshot, or even fainting. There are a variety of techniques that can work depending on the abilities and physique of a given actor. However, any technique used should be capable of being performed at nearly any tempo, be easily adaptable in a variety of dramatic or comedic situations, and be repeatable to a degree that any chance of injury is virtually eliminated.

We used to fall all the time as toddlers. When attempting to walk we would struggle to get up and typically go right back to the ground again. As we have matured and started to socialize, the embarrassment attached to falling down becomes ever more present. Only the young and inexperienced fall since they are not in control of their bodies. One of the marks of adulthood is to be able to stand and be in control. But in this quest for adult control we have lost the sensibility of how to take care of ourselves when a fall inevitably happens. Falling from a standing position because of any kind of imbalance can be scary but it does not have to be so. If we allow our bodies to remember how to handle to impact, the fall will no longer cause so much panic.

This following exercise is also a good one for helping the performer explore his or her attitudes towards falling. Most people are scared of falling. And why not? Falling is seldom associated with good images. Usually people get hurt or worse from falling. However, the act of falling in and of itself will not injure a human body. The impact, or more precisely the sudden deceleration, of the human body is the cause of injury. The fall will and can cause a lot of anxiety especially if the fall is from a great height (a common guideline for determining whether or not a descent counts as a "high fall" is to multiply the height of the person by 3 or any fall that measures 15 feet from the point of where the feet are on the platform to the ground). Unless you are performing for a stunt show or Cirque du Soleil, chances are slim that you will have to deal with a high fall during a show. However, falls from the standing position are quite common no matter what the production. Here the issue of injury becomes not really about sudden deceleration (although we must always be aware of the fact conceptually) but rather how the performer can disperse the energy of impact so that the possibility of injury is minimized. The most important thing, as usual, is to relax and use only the muscles necessary to efficiently disperse energy after a fall. Remember, it's not falling that hurts. It's all the things that we do to keep from falling that cause problems.

To begin to understand what is involved in the act of falling one should investigate what it is like for the human body to be imbalanced. This kind of investigation can be easily made with a simple exercise. Begin by standing in a relaxed position with the knees bent and the feet parallel. Slowly rock forward onto the balls of the feet and then back on the heels. Feel the distribution of weight as it shifts forward back. Now rock from side to side on the inside and outside of the feet. Get a feel for where your center of gravity is and how you can manipulate it given the position of your feet. Now begin to lean forward to test the limits of your balance in that direction. When you feel that you are about to fall allow yourself to keep leaning forward until you must catch yourself by making a big step forward with either the left or right leg (Figures 14.1–14.6). You can also perform this exercise in any direction (backwards, to the side on a 90-degree angle, or on diagonal angles) to further explore how you can perceive and handle imbalances in the body.

14.1

14.2

14.3

14.4

14.5

14.6

Return to the imbalance moving forward in the big step. In order to fall forward we can use the beginning of this one big step to access the first technique. When you catch yourself with the big step or lunge see if you can keep your balance there. Alter the position of your front foot so that the width distance between your front and back foot is not too narrow. It should almost feel as though you are lunging slightly to the side while keeping a fair amount of space between your legs. Now reach out with both hands in the space between your feet and turn your head to look in the direction of your bent knee that is forward. As your center lowers to the ground, contact the floor with your hands and bend at the elbows as though the arms were shock absorbers on a car. This will be useful in controlling your descent to the floor (think of it as though you were going to do a push-up). Make sure that every part of the anterior of the body arrives at the same time, taking special care to not knock hips and knees on the floor. The initial position on the floor should look as though you were crawling across the floor for an instant. When the entire body reaches the floor relax the arms and legs to assume whatever prone position is most appropriate for that moment (Figures 14.7–14.11). This is commonly referred to as the *front fall*.

14.7

14.8

14.9

14.10

14.11

To fall backwards (*back fall or sit fall*) requires some slight alterations to this technique since the direction of the fall has obviously changed. (Look at the Drunken Sailor exercise in Chapter 9 Games to warm up on the mechanics of this technique.) From the standing position take a big step with either the right or left foot but this time step backwards. You will find yourself in a similar lunge position to that used in the front fall. The position of the feet should allow for room to exist between the legs so as to maintain lateral stability through the technique. Reach out the arms to counter balance the weight that is travelling backwards (these arms can also be used to splay out for dramatic effect once the technique is proficient). Now relax the knees and roll through the legs while making a smooth, diagonal descent to the floor (Figures 14.12–14.17).

It should be noted that at no time should the arms reach back to assist in "catching" the fall. All too often this is the human reaction to falling backwards. It is one of the few human instincts that actually does us no good. The arms are meant to articulate towards the anterior of the body. Once the shoulders rotate the arms towards the posterior, that mobility is severely limited. As a result, any "catching" of the fall that occurs when falling backwards usually happens with the arms in a locked position. Any force that is received by the arms

14.12

14.13

14.14

14.15

at this point will transfer to the weakest most delicate points of the arm – the joints. The probability of sustaining a joint injury in the wrist, elbows, or shoulder skyrockets if the arms are not reaching up and away during this technique. A good reminder to ensure that the arms reach forward and not back is to reach towards the thing or person who was the cause of the fall.

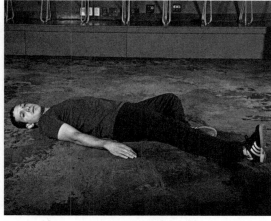

14.16

Sometimes one needs to fall to the ground in a confined area. Here it is impossible to take a big step either forward or backward to do the above techniques. In this instance the performer can execute a *twist fall*. The performer begins with the feet shoulder width apart and parallel to one another. The body rotates at the point of contact from the force that causes the fall. As this twist initiates, there is a corkscrewing motion of the body as the hips lower to the floor. The knees should bend and the knees end up crossing like a pretzel as the hips

14.17

14.18

14.19

14.20

meet the floor. When the backside meets the floor the performer then rolls through the spine in much the same way as the back fall and extends the energy out of the legs to end up in the supine position. The final position on the floor is typically facing 180 degrees in the opposite direction of when the twist fall had begun. However, depending on the needs of staging, force of the blow leading into the fall, and the flexibility of the performer the final position can be adjusted to any desired orientation (Figures 14.21–14.24).

14.21

14.22

14.23

14.24

Assassin

This is a game to reinforce the techniques of going to the ground. It is modeled on the classic game by the same name. One person in a group is silently chosen to be the assassin. Once the game begins everyone in the group walks about the space and greets anyone they come in proximity to. This is done with a handshake (in some versions of the game it is simply with eye contact). If the assassin shakes hands with a person in the group the assassin has a choice of either letting the person go or touching the person's wrist with the forefinger of the right hand. If the latter happens the person has been "marked" and must shake at least two other peoples' hands before dying. The person who dies must go to the ground using one of the techniques listed above. If someone has a notion of whom the assassin is then that person must say, "J'accuse!" If the accuser is right then they win and get to choose the next assassin for the next game. If they are wrong then they must go to jail and observe the game for the rest of the round and cannot be the assassin for the next game. The assassin wins when the entirety of the group is either dead or in jail.

CONTROLLING ACTIONS

Something typically required of actors in many scenes is to physically control the other actor. That may be an action to keep someone in the room by grabbing them, dislodge them from the space by pushing them, or trying to make them submit by causing pain such as grabbing of the hair or choking. All of these moves have their own advantages and challenges as techniques. Above all, each one requires close enough proximity between the actors so that actual contact can be made. In fact, the closer the performers are to one another during these techniques the more playable the moments become and also the less likely the chances for injury. To review the concepts at work in these techniques refer to Chapter 13 Contact Violence.

Pushing

The push is perhaps the most basic and most misinterpreted move in enacting violence for theatre. The pitfalls here are that the performers who rush into the push do not bother to match either the force or timing of the push. Both must be mutually agreed upon by both performers for the push to be visually sound and affecting for the audience. Pushes can happen from anywhere on the operator's body to anywhere on the receiver's body really. The optimal and most likely combination of places is when the hand or hands of the operator are placed on the torso of the receiver. The force created from this particular combination creates an imbalance in the receiver that is playable for a scene with violent conflict.

The optimal locations to place one or both hands on the torso are the upper pectorals below the collarbone. This location satisfies the guidelines for making contact with a large muscle group and still gives the operator the solid structure of the thoracic region to push against (Figures 14.25–14.27). Make certain that the push does not migrate up towards the collarbone or out towards the shoulder joints as putting too much force on these less supported structures can lead to bruising and injury. Another viable location for the push would be placing the hand or hands on the major muscles of the upper back such as the trapezius or rhomboids between the shoulder blades and spine. Both of these locations provide good contact for both performers to have playable transfer of energy without increasing the risk of injury to bones, joints, or soft tissue if the force is increased (Figures 14.28–14.30). Also, the push can be executed from a variety of staging options depending on if the operator of the push is placed in front or behind of the receiver. The deltoid or shoulder muscle on the upper arms is another location where the push can be located. This is a good variation to practice since both performers can execute the technique while standing next to each other in a scene (Figures 14.31–14.33). Here since the deltoid is located between the shoulder and elbow joints extra care should be taken to avoid these structures as additional force here has a higher likelihood of resulting in discomfort or injury.

A push from the front, one handed:

14.25

14.26

14.27

A push from the back:

14.28

14.29

14.30

A push from the side:

14.31

14.32

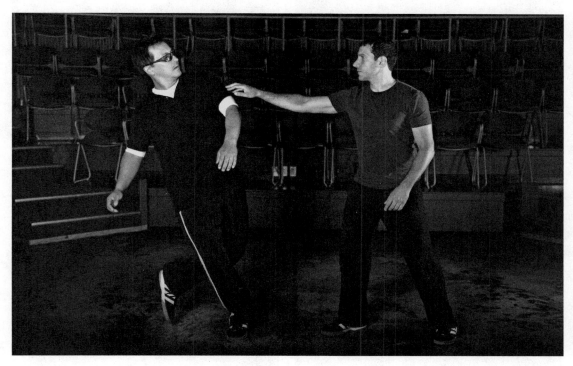

14.33

A push from the front, two handed:

14.34

14.35

14.36

14.37

14.38

The receiver should respond only to the amount of force that the operator has given. Experiment with different levels of force using the 1–10 scale to see which amount of force is most comfortable for the performers and most appropriate for the interaction of the characters.

Grabbing

Usually when a person grabs onto another person it is done circumferentially around a limb such as the arm or leg (controlling grabs can be done around the neck as well but this is covered more specifically later on when describing choking techniques). All of the fingers wrap around a limb creating a controlling circle to complete the grab. While grabbing in this way will prove effective the problem becomes possible discomfort through point pressure transferred to the receiver of the action. There are admittedly other techniques out there such as the "bracelet hold" (which makes a circle around the limb but does not squeeze the limb) as well as others that rely on quality of touch to guard against transferring too much pressure to the receiver. However, I have found that in the heat of performance, no matter what the level of training or technique, it is next to impossible not to grab another human being without some transference of force, particularly when the performer is really intent on and connected to the action. If this is done with the fingers and thumb in a traditional position for a grab then the change of point pressure and bruising to musculature and soft tissue of the receiver increases dramatically.

14.39

14.40

14.41

14.42

Rather than use the thumb to grab on stage, wed the thumb to the other four fingers and think about using the hand as a "slap bracelet." As the hand contacts the area to be grabbed, say the wrist, the fingers wrap around the wrist but do not connect to the thumb since it is alongside the fingers (Figures 14.39–14.40). This allows the receiver to break free at any time. Of course this could cause a problem to the violent interaction since the receiver is actually not being controlled in this moment. To make the grab effective, the receiver must actually pull in the direction of the palm of the operator, not in the direction of the space (Figure 14.41). While the specific body part, usually the forearm or upper arm, moves in the direction of the grabbing palm, the rest of the body must move in the opposite direction of the grab (Figure 14.42). This dynamic tension will create the visual picture that the person being grabbed does not want to be grabbed. This gives both performers a moment of real, playable opposition through the grab.

In order to "break" the hold, the receiver simply changes the direction of the force being put into the grabbing palm to just outside the fingertips of that palm. This will allow the receiver to "escape" the hold easily. However, the receiver should not simply slip out of the hold without effort. When the direction of the force is changed the receiver can give a pulse to the action as though he or she were breaking free from the grab. The operator can then extend the grabbing arm to follow the receiver's motion as though the receiver actually broke the hold. This will give the illusion that effort was expended in escaping the hold.

Restraining

In order to restrain a performer it is important to first position yourself in front of the actor to be restrained. Too many actors try to intercept their friends from behind before going into the restraint. This is not only ineffective but it is also probably not connected to the true intent of the scene. Once the performer to be restrained makes a move to leave, or threatens someone else on stage, the person to do the restraining must move his or her feet and get in front of the person to be restrained. Only then can the operator use his or her body to physically impede the receiver and move into the rest of the technique.

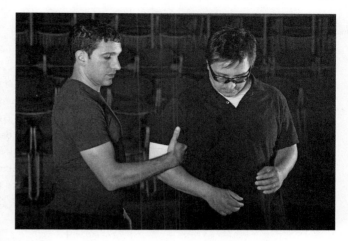

14.43

- Grab the receiver by the bicep with the slap bracelet hold (Figure 14.43).
- Step into the receiver so that the hips of the two partners are touching. There should be no space between the hips. This is important to allow good kinesthetic response between the two actors if there is to be a struggle during the restraining.
- The non-grabbing hand of the operator should be active and grab the opposing shoulder or bicep of the receiver's other arm (Figure 14.44).
- Snake the initial grabbing arm between the bicep and the back of the receiver to increase the connection.
- Struggle as necessary. Keep in mind not to be bogus about it. Any struggling should be with as much force and energy as both performers are comfortable using. Also, the force being used should have a specific intent: to keep someone in the room, to escape to safety, etc.

14.44

14.45

Clothing Grab

The entry for this technique is similar to the first part of the technique for pushing. The palm of the hand or hands seeks out the upper pectorals (Figure 14.46). Make certain that the entering palm is flat as possible upon contact. The clothing underneath the palm is collected between the thumb and forefinger of the operator's hand (Figure 14.47). The rest of the hand closes into a fist collecting additional fabric along the way (Figure 14.48). The position of the fist echoes the positions appropriate for striking. Only flat surfaces should be used to rest against the chest of the receiver. If the knuckles are grinding into the pectorals then readjust the position of the fists until the point pressure disappears (Figures 14.49–14.52).

14.46

14.47

14.48

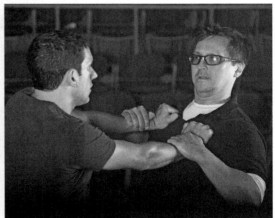

14.49

When the operator has fully grasped the material the receiver should grab the operator's forearms (see grabbing above for appropriate technique). This grab should be done in such a way that the fists of the operator are brought into the chest of the receiver thereby creating solid contact between the two. The performers should feel as though the fists are sealed or suction cupped to the pectorals in such a way that if the bodies move then the fists remain exactly in place on the upper chest.

14.50

14.51

14.52

Obviously, shirts with a bit more material and with a heavier more resilient fabric are ideal for grabbing in this way. Jackets with lapels are ideal. This move should be executed with care when tight fitting shirts or tops with delicate material are involved. If this is the case then another controlling technique should be employed to minimize the risk of damaging the costume.

14.53

Hair Grab

Of all the stage combat techniques this one is probably the most popular and the most infamous. Oftentimes what happens when hair is about to be pulled in a scene, the operator makes a fist and places it on top of the receiver's head. The receiver then grabs on to the operator's fist thereby attaching it to the head. Then the receiver starts flailing around. This manifestation of the technique has always been disappointing to watch since there is little physical connectivity where the actors can effectively kinesthetically respond to one another. Also this version of the technique is so far from the reality of grabbing hair it borders on the absurd. Most people have their thickest portion of hair near the back of the head, not at the top. If someone were really intent on controlling another person by the hair they would most likely go for the region of the head that has the most hair to latch on to.

- For a hair pull when approaching from the front contact the upper pectorals with an open palm. Slide up the chest and over the shoulder while supinating the hand with the palm up. The back of the forearm of the operator should be nestled comfortably and solidly on the upper pectoral of the receiver. This contact should remain consistent throughout the technique (Figures 14.54–14.57).

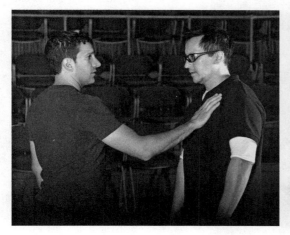

14.54

14.55

14.56

14.57

14.58

- For a hair pull from the rear contact the upper back with the same open palm. Slide the hand up the back to the crown of the head. The front of the forearm of the operator should be placed comfortably and solidly on the upper back of the receiver. This contact should remain consistent throughout the technique (Figures 14.58–14.60).

14.59

14.60

- Have the hand move to the back of the head while crooking the hand to gather some hair between the fingers. At this point some hair should be visible between the fingers to show that the hair is actually being collected in the hand (Figure 14.61).

14.61

- Use the other hand to hold on to the receiver's arm or waist for further control.
- When marking a moment where the "grab" turns into a "pull" simply pulse the arm involved in the hair grab. The receiver should feel this pulse and respond with a sharp upward motion in the direction of the hair accompanied by a sharp yelp.
- Please do not simply thrash around during the hair pull. The receiver should not move until the operator gives the pulse. Both performers should remember to keep the heads and torsos upright so that any spoken text can be more easily heard (Figure 14.62).

14.62

Choking

Of all of the techniques available to a performer, the act of choking or being choked is one of the most playable and dramatically affecting for both the actors and the audience. The close proximity of the characters required during the technique helps make this an intensely intimate moment. Also the experience of having lost the capacity to breathe is one that is immediately accessible for any observer. The viewer may not have a direct experience of being choked or choking someone but everyone has had the experience of having difficulty breathing whether from illness, being underwater for too long, or having pressure on any part of the respiratory system. Also, while few people may have had the actual experience of wrapping hands or arms around another human being's airway I have found that when someone has posed the question of if they have ever thought about choking someone a lot of people have admitted to having that dark thought even fleetingly at one time or another. While the physical reality of following through with this intent is not as common the emotional and psychological understanding of the motivation behind it is something most people seem to connect to.

For the actor, the psychological barriers inherent in performing this technique may be very strong, and with good cause. The neck is an extremely sensitive and personal area with many vital structures imperative to breathing, circulation, mobility, and sensation. The trachea (or windpipe) at the front of the throat needs to stay intact for normal breathing to occur. The carotid arteries on the sides of the neck bring oxygenated blood from the heart to the brain. The spinal cord in the back of the neck acts as what F. Matthais Alexander (creator of the famed Alexander Technique widely used to great effect by artists to find ease in their work through removing habitual patterns of moving and thinking) called the "primary control." This portion of the spinal column is involved in enervating the rest of the body. There are many possibilities for injury when directing force towards the neck. Both performers must be rigorous and mindful when practicing and performing any technique that involves choking for stage.

14.63   14.64

14.65

14.66

- For the *front choke* the first entry point for this technique is like those that have come before – flat palms against the upper pectoral. This allows the operator of the choke to put more energy into the beginning of the move as opposed to going straight for the soft tissue of the throat, which cannot take as much force as the solid structure of the torso (Figure 14.63–14.64).
- The hands should start to change shape as shown in Figure 14.67. The four fingers come together and should fan out to form a "C." As the hands slide up to the neck, the pinky side of the hand and heels of the palms should rest on the upper torso of the receiver while the ridge created by the index finger and thumb provides a shelf on which the receiver can rest his or her mandible (jaw) (Figures 14.67–14.68).

14.67

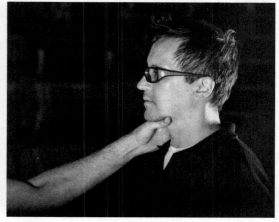

14.68

14.69

14.70

- One hand or both hands may be used for this technique. If one hand is used, the space shown in Figure 14.68 should be placed on the upstage side of the audience so as not to show any space between the operator's hand and the receiver's throat. If both hands are used (Figure 14.69) then the thumb of one hand should overlap the large knuckle of the index finger of the opposite hand, as in Figure 14.70. The other thumb should disappear underneath the large knuckle of the index finger of the first hand. The shape made by both hands should look like a "V." At no time should the thumbs infringe on the space in front of the throat.

- As the operator is arriving in this position the receiver should be animating his or her body and hands to demonstrate that he or she presumably does not want to be choked. Even though the gesture with the hands should suggest this, in actuality the actor can use this gesture to initiate contact with the operator in order to comfortably position the hands for the choke. The receiver gasps the forearms of the operator and tucks the chin to create a good seal between the jaw and the ridge of the hands and also between the pinky side of the hands and the upper torso.

- It should be noted that maintaining tight, consistent contact between performers on this move is of paramount importance. Tight contact not only allows the illusion that the hands are tightly wound around the throat to continue it also allows those hands to serve as a stabilizing device for the neck of the receiver. This keeps the cervical spine in line and minimizes the chance of injury when more energy is put into the technique.

- Energy is and should be put into the technique. The energy does not and should not go into the soft tissue of the neck. The fingers can be curled to simulate this but extra care should be taken that point pressure is not used on any portion of the neck. Any and all energy of this move should be directed through the heel of the palms of the operator. The heel of the palms should be flush against the chest of the receiver. Pulses can be used against the chest in such a way to show energy being transferred through the action. The receiver then takes that energy and translates it through manipulating breath and sound to give the illusion of being choked.

- Different hand positions for the receiver can be used as well in this technique (Figures 14.71–14.72). No matter what the changing position through the struggle of the choke one hand or arm should always be able to keep the seal between the hands, jaw, and chest tight. This allows more mobility for both performers during the technique and even allows the performers the ability to take the action to the ground if necessary. If this does happen it should be rehearsed in a way that both performers are balanced at every moment through the transition to the floor. At no time should the performers feel as though either one is falling to the ground during this technique.

14.71

14.72

- Performing a *back choke* or *rear choke* has many similarities to the front choke. The entry this time is from behind the receiver (Figure 14.73). The non-choking hand of the operator is placed on the shoulder of the receiver as a preparatory beat to make certain the receiver is ready (Figure 14.74). The hand of the choking arm is placed on the upper back on the opposite side and slid over the opposing shoulder, across the chest, and to the same shoulder where the non-choking hand originally made contact (Figures 14.75–14.76).

14.73

14.74

14.75

14.76

- During this action, the hips and torso of both performers should come together with one leg of the operator between the legs of the receiver. This leg should be bent slightly so as to allow a ledge on which the receiver may sit and balance (Figure 14.77).

- The receiver animates his or her arms in a similar fashion as with the front choke to help place the arm in a comfortable position on the upper torso. The elbow of the choking arm should ideally be under the receiver's chin creating a "V" with the arm similar to the "V" created by the hands in the front choke. However, for some actors with broader shoulders this may be an impossible position to achieve. In this case simply placing the forearm across the upper chest will suffice. Extra care should then be taken not to place the forearm directly against the trachea (Figure 14.78).

14.77

- The receiver should then tuck the chin and make sure the same tight seal is created between the jaw, arm, and upper torso.

- Any struggling that happens here should occur through pulses directed down and into the sternum of the receiver. Make sure not to flex the muscles of the arm too much around the neck as that will turn this stage combat technique into a real choking technique and interrupt the blood flow through the carotid arteries to the brain. Constant verbal communication between partners during rehearsal should be practiced at all times.

- The hips of both performers should be in contact at all times. If the receiver should buck out the hips at any time this will put undue extension force on the cervical spine and possibly result in a major injury. Keep the hips together!

14.78

- For those performers who are very tall and need to be choked by a shorter partner, starting from a kneeling position is also a good way to perform this technique. Here the whole body of the shorter performer acts as a backstop against which the taller receiver can struggle.

14.79

14.80

14.81

14.82

- Remember during the choke the receiver is trying to breathe. Many people choose to cough while performing this technique. This breath pattern is actually the body clearing the airway. Here the performer should explore making breath sounds in a rhythm and fashion that suggest a restricted airway. Gasping and an interrupted, staccato breath pattern is more in line with exploring the reality of this technique.

Biting

Biting is a less often used technique but can be very effective when the fight calls for a more scrappy quality. Even though the teeth are not used in this technique, the best location for the bite is to a clothed muscle group on the receiver. Less muscled or bare areas of the body tend to have less cushioning for the jaws to settle comfortably. Clothing also acts as a barrier for any slobber that might result from the technique.

14.83

- At the most closely available muscled area on the receiver (in the case Figure 14.83, the upper arm) the operator opens his or her mouth wide to bare the teeth (Figure 14.84). This is an important part of the technique as it demonstrates clearly the intent of the operator to bite the receiver. Without this moment before the bite it leaves the audience to surmise what occurred through solely the reaction of the receiver. Baring the teeth initially completes the lines of action for the audience to clearly follow.
- As the mouth is brought closer to the area in one swift action the operator covers the teeth with his or her lips to prevent him or herself from actually placing the teeth on the body of the receiver. The operator must be sensitive to his or her own lips so as not to apply too much force and bite his or her own lips (Figure 14.85).
- The receiver should respond vocally to the bite (typically with a vocalization using the higher register) but stay in contact with the operator for at least 2 seconds. If the receiver pulls away too soon the dramatic effect of the bite is typically not as great.

14.84

14.85

STRIKING

Slaps

The slap is quite possibly the most underestimated technique in all of stagecraft. It appears in countless shows whether written expressly by the playwright or added into the staging by the director or the actors. While the emotional concept of the slap is immediately recognized by nearly anyone, the physical realities are often greatly misunderstood. A true slap is a strike to the head and as such carries with it the same dangers as any other mode of force being transferred to the head. Additionally, there are other concerns for the receiver such as fingers clipping the eyes, nose, or mouth. Also, an open palm contacting the ear with force creates a rush of air within the ear canal that will likely damage the eardrum either temporarily or permanently leading to partial or total hearing loss in that ear. Distance, timing, and accurate targeting are of paramount importance in the execution of this technique.

Forehand Slap (performance angle shown)

14.86

14.87

14.88

14.89

- While this technique can be done at a variety of distances between partners the best results typically occur when the actors are far enough away from each other that at the moment of greatest extension of the operator's slapping arm the fingers of that hand are approximately 6 inches from the tip of the receiver's nose. This distance gives the operator a greater sense of freedom of movement without endangering the receiver. From this position the receiver can more freely alter the speed and force of the swing to find more nuance and accuracy for the moment of the strike. Of course, the distance can be lessened between the performers and the hit still be valid. However, this shortening of the distance requires the operator to bend the hitting arm. In my experience, this shortening of the arm leads to a more controlled swing since both operator and receiver feel the proximity more acutely. A more controlled swing leads to less freedom of movement and not as much availability to adjust speed and force during the hit (Figures 14.90–14.93 – open angle).

14.90

14.91

14.92

14.93

- The operator and the receiver should position themselves in the *offset* position and not be stacked – the operator lined up with the receiver's left shoulder for a right-handed forehand slap or lined up with the receiver's right shoulder for a left-handed forehand slap.
- The striking hand should be open and relaxed, not rigid. As the motion is initiated the hand should travel in a straight line on a horizontal plane in front of the nose of the receiver. This necessitates the hand being raised up first rather than throwing the hand up from the hip.
- The target of the slap should always travel through the space directly in front of the tip of the receiver's nose. This may seem like it is a bit too high since the intended target should be the cheek. However, when the cheek is targeted the audience typically views the hit as connecting more with the neck than the face. To adjust this difference in perception the target for slaps, punches, and most non-contact strikes to the head should be targeted with the tip of the nose as the center point.
- The action of the arm and hand should have the feeling of a free and easy swing. However, since we are attempting to create the illusion of the hand striking a solid object there must also be an interruption in the path of the technique. If this does not occur it may seem as though the hand simply passes through thin air thereby breaking the illusion of violence. A way to add in the impression of contact is to add a *pulse* at the moment where the fingers pass in front of the nose. This pulse is similar to the pulses referred to in previous techniques. It is a momentary activation of the muscles of the arm and hand. This distance that allows full extension of this technique also enables the operator to more easily add in the pulse. Some images that may assist in adding in the pulse are shaking or flicking water off the ends of the fingers into the face of the receiver. Or as a former student suggested, imagine you have all the anger associated with the technique in a flame in your hand. The moment of impact is when you "throw the fire."
- The moment of the pulse is when the receiver should turn his or her head in the appropriate direction of the strike with a reaction that matches the force of the operator's action. This is also when the knap occurs.
- It is important that as many audience members see the beginning, middle, and end of the strike as possible. After the moment of the strike and knap the operator must continue the line of the strike for as long as is naturally possible. This extension of the line of the strike will enable the strike to read as a hit to as many audience perspectives as possible.
- Not all strikes need be horizontal. Some can be ascending diagonally or descending diagonally. Each of these particular changes in direction of the action must be accompanied by a change in reaction by the receiver (see artist renderings of different head reactions, Figure 14.94). A change in direction of the strike will change the intent of the violence. Both operator and receiver should agree on the direction of the strike so that the action and reaction can be accurately executed. **Watch the videos on the companion website to see how an observer may get a different idea about the relationship between the two characters based on the different directions of the slaps.**
- As always make sure to open up the picture after the slap has occurred.

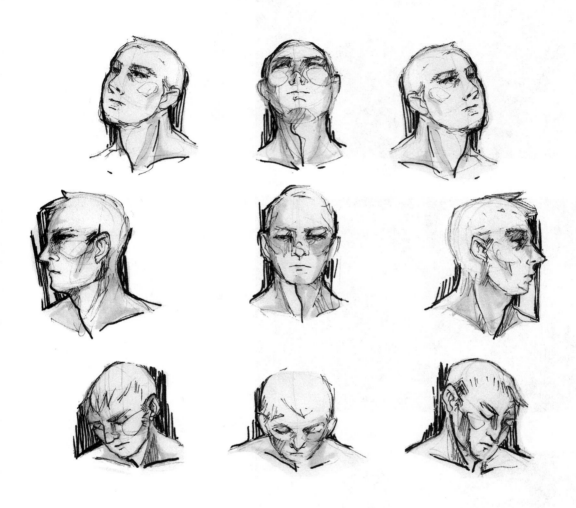

14.94

14.95

14.96

14.97

Backhand Slap

• The backhand slap can be done in a nearly identical way to the forehand slap. This time since the contacting surface should be the back of the hand, the operator must line up over the receiver's right shoulder. The direction of the strike may be horizontal, ascending diagonal, or descending diagonal travelling through the space in front of the tip of the nose and extending the line for as long as is naturally possible. The receiver makes a clap knap and reacts in a way that is commensurate with the force of the attack. Figures 14.95–14.97 show an ascending backhand slap at performance angle.

- Another variation of the backhand slap involves a shared knap rather than a clap knap. For the shared knap backhand the best direction of the strike to ensure a solid knap is in the ascending diagonal direction. At this angle the back of the hand of the operator can meet the palm of the receiver perpendicularly to achieve maximum sound for the knap. Once again the line of the backhand must be extended for the hit to read. The reaction of the receiver should be up and away in the direction of the ascending diagonal (in the case of a right-handed backhand the receiver would react up and to the left). Figures 14.98–14.100 show an ascending shared backhand slap at open angle.

14.98

14.99

14.100

In-the-round Slap or V-slap (performance angle)

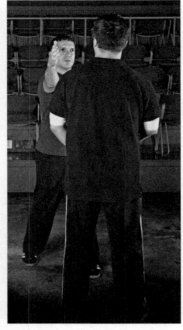

14.101

14.102

14.103

14.104

This slap is necessary for any actor who works in non-proscenium spaces where the audience can be on multiple sides of the playing space, particularly in-the-round or thrust spaces. It is also useful for slaps that for staging purposes must be done with the characters in profile to the audience. This technique will feel very unnatural and non-impulsive in practice since the path of the hand does not follow one path but rather two. However, with dedicated rehearsal time this technique can become a powerful tool to make a slap read with any kind of staging.

14.105

14.106

14.107

14.108

- As with the forehand slap this technique will begin with the performers standing in the offset position. The performers will be *in distance* for this technique, close enough for the operator to completely rest his or her hand on the left shoulder of the receiver.
- For a right-handed slap the hand should be raised to the level of the intended target, i.e. the receiver's left cheek. The right elbow should be at least parallel with the floor at a 90-degree angle (or even a little higher) with the palm of the hand facing out and in front of the operator.
- The first action path of the hand is not across but rather straight out to a place in space over the point of the left shoulder of the receiver. The palm should rotate through this path to face the cheek of the receiver with the fingers pointed past the receiver's shoulder at the moment of greatest extension for the operator. From the profile view the hand should completely disappear behind the head of the receiver or completely cover the side of the receiver's face. This part of the technique covers the target from the profile view (Figures 14.109–14.112 show performance angle).
- After the moment of greatest extension (which should include the *pulse* mentioned previously) the operator will then drop the right elbow to allow the right palm to rotate so that the fingers point up to the ceiling. The path of the hand should travel on an acute angle to the initial direction of the technique making a "V" or check-mark like path to completion. This part of the technique covers the target from other audience angles.

14.109

14.110

14.111

14.112

- For the second part of the "V" path the hand of the operator should cross the centerline of the receiver right in front of the tip of the nose. The palm should be towards the face of the receiver with the fingers pointing up to the ceiling. Make certain not to point the fingertips across the face of the receiver. Being in distance this might put the receiver in danger of being scratched or worse.
- Finally, the hand of the operator should end past his or her own left shoulder with the palm facing out.

It should be noted that with this technique the accent of the action should be after the moment of greatest extension by the arm of the operator. Just after this moment, the operator should slightly increase the velocity of the pullback to complete the illusion of this slap. Also note that this slap cannot be performed as a backhand. The mechanics of the arms simply won't allow it.

PUNCHES

It will be the rare (and perhaps wonderfully lucky) occasion where an actor will play a character that is a trained fighter. As a result, most of the punches used in theatre and film will require an untrained quality to them. However, this does not mean that the shape or action of the punch can be sloppy. Every punching technique still must be precise in shape and trajectory in order to communicate that this strike, unlike the slap, is meant to cause damage. (For a description of how to properly shape the fist for these punching techniques refer to Chapter 13 Contact Violence.)

The Roundhouse Punch or Haymaker

This is the bread-and-butter punch for any situation of violence that calls for an untrained yet powerful and emotional hit. The name of this punch is derived from the motion that it makes. The fist will travel in a semicircular fashion around the space in between the performers that also mimics the action of cutting hay with a scythe. The wide arcing action of the punch enables the technique to cover many angles and also enables the performer to fully commit to a large, wild motion (Figure 14.113).

14.113

As with the forehand slap this technique will begin with the performers standing in the offset position. The rest of the technique is identical to the steps outlined for the *forehand slap*. All of the notes on distance, targeting, pulsing, etc. apply to this technique as well. The only differences to this technique are the following:

- The hand of the operator is now in the shape of a fist instead of an open palm.
- The receiver will more likely make a body knap instead of a clap knap to differentiate the sound of a punch from a slap. There are of course always exceptions to this. If the receiver is heavily clothed in such a way that muffles any possible sound for the body knap then a clap knap should be used. Also, clap knaps tend to carry more in larger playing spaces because of the high quality of the pitch generated. If the body knap is too soft, a clap knap should be used for maximum theatrical effect.

14.114

14.115

14.116

14.117

- In order to communicate to the audience that the operator has delivered a more powerful strike, the rotation of the hips in the direction of the motion of the punch will aid in this. Make sure that when the hips are rotated in this way that the torso remains upright. Bending at the waist will diminish the perceived power of the strike. It will also diminish the higher status of the operator who successfully punched the receiver. And finally, it will prohibit the audience from seeing the face of the operator since he or she will most likely be facing the floor as a result.
- Since punches are usually delivered with more powerful intent, the receiver must react in a more forcefully commensurate way from this action. A good knap and a sharp reaction will go a long way here to complete the illusion. Figures 14.114–14.117 show the roundhouse performance angle.

Like the forehand slap the roundhouse punch can be delivered from multiple angles depending on the difference in height of the two performers or the intended effect of the punch. This punch can also be delivered in the same fashion as the non-contact *backhand slap*. In this case the punch would then be referred to as a *backfist*. Figures 14.118–14.121 show the open angle.

14.118

14.119

14.120

14.121

The Cross or Straight Punch

This punch is most commonly used as an alternative to the roundhouse punch when the character doing the punching needs to demonstrate skill. The cross or straight right derives its name from the path it takes through space. It is delivered from the rear hand in such a way that it travels across the body of the operator and the target of the receiver in a straight line. The main difference in this technique to the roundhouse is that the cross or straight punch travels in a linear path parallel to the target (the head of the receiver). This change in the flight path of the strike from a semicircle to a straight line communicates a focused directionality of the strike. This focus in a linear direction will help an audience believe that the operator has some skill in striking with the fist (Figure 14.122).

14.122

- As with the forehand slap and roundhouse punch this technique will begin with the performers standing in the offset position. Here it is important for the operator to step slightly forward with the foot on the same side of the hand doing the strike (the right foot for a right cross, the left foot for a left cross). This orientation of the feet allows the hips to release in the direction of the strike. This allows for more articulation of the body to deliver power and extend the line to cover the target for multiple angles. To do this the operator must pivot on the ball of the right foot (in much the same way for the twisting of the body at the beginning of the warm-up) and allow the hips to turn in the intended direction of the strike.
- The fist should be raised in such a way that it is at the same level as the head of the receiver. The knuckles of the fist should *not* be pointed towards the receiver's head. Rather the knuckles of the fist should be pointed on a track through space parallel to the head of the receiver. This path should shoot the fist and arm like an arrow parallel to the head of the receiver passing through the space 6 inches from the tip of the receiver's nose (Figures 14.123–14.126 – performance angle).

14.123

14.124

14.125

14.126

- If there is a major difference in height of the performers the receiver can lower his or her head by rounding the shoulders and hunching the back or naturally bending the knees so that the level of the entire body drops. Also, the operator can change to a slightly ascending angle of the cross if the target is still too high to naturally make the punch horizontal. If this is the case then the receiver must react in the direction that is commensurate with the angle of the punch.
- The line of the punch must be extended in such a way so that the fist appears on the other side of the receiver's head. This long line to the cross not only demonstrates a stronger intent but it also covers the target for a wider angle of audience perspective (Figures 14.127–14.130 – open angle).
- At the end of the punch, keep the body upright and simply relax the arm down as the receiver vacates the area. Do not snap the arm and fist back the same way it just travelled. This action may break the illusion of the technique.
- Like the roundhouse punch, the receiver should use a body knap and react with the vigour of being clocked in the face.

14.127

14.128

14.129

14.130

One of the marvelous benefits of this particular technique is that it can be performed equally well with the receiver being downstage or upstage of the operator. If the receiver is unable to knap or the staging requires the receiver to be upstage then this technique is very conducive to allowing the operator to both punch and knap *at the same time*. This is known as a *self knap*. This is achieved by following the steps listed above almost identically. During the set-up of the punch the left hand of the operator should reach out naturally as though to counter balance the motion of preparing the punch. When the operator turns the hips in the direction of the strike, the shoulders should follow suit. As the fist travels through the path parallel to the target, the left hand should be travelling towards the right pectoral muscle of the operator. The operator should time the sound of the knap when the fist is directly in front of the nose of the receiver. After the strike is complete the knap hand should relax back into a fist to a position away from the location of the knap so as not to draw attention to where the knap was performed. This is a versatile technique that when mastered can be used in multiple situations or performer orientations.

The Jab

This technique is another example of a punch that can be thrown with the receiver in the upstage position. The jab is traditionally a punch that is thrown off of the lead hand. It is a sharp, quick punch that usually stuns an opponent but lacks the power of the roundhouse or cross. For this technique it is the quality of the jab that is referenced rather than the accurate physical definition since here the jab will be thrown with the rear hand.

14.131

14.132

14.133

- Set up in the offset position except this time if the jab is to be thrown with the right hand the operator should be in line with the receiver's right, not the left shoulder as in previous techniques. Also, the operator's left foot should be placed slightly ahead of his or her right foot.
- It is very important that the head or target of the receiver should be clearly visible to the center mass of the audience. If using this technique for film the face of the receiver should be in clear view of the camera (Figures 14.132–14.133 – performance angle).
- Keeping a bent arm with the elbow at an approximate 90-degree angle, the operator should shrug the right shoulder into the punch and place the fist in a quick, sharp motion at a point 6 inches in front of the receiver's face. The arm should never be fully extended in this technique.

- At the moment the fist reaches that position in space the operator performs a self knap in the same fashion as one may do for the cross.
- The fist should have a quality of bouncing off of the head as the fist returns to the relaxed original position (Figures 14.134–14.135 – open angle).
- The reaction of the receiver should be simple and stunned. Since the direction of this strike is straight into the face, the reaction of the head is down and in, not up. A head reaction that travels up should be reserved for rising roundhouses or crosses. The reaction to the jab should be akin to nodding the head upon hearing the knap. (Think of it as your inner monologue response to the action, "Yes, you just popped me in the face.")

14.134

14.135

- Since this technique is on-line directly to the receiver's face it is of the utmost importance that the operator never gets any closer than 6 inches. With this particular set-up the operator should have a clear view of the space in between when the punch is placed and the receiver's face (Figures 14.136–14.137 – open angle).

The jab is quick and can have a nice sudden effect but it is difficult to master. The most difficult part is finding exactly the right placement for the fist in front of the face to cover the target from a variety of angles. Depending on the placement on stage for the actors, the exact placement of the punch should change. For actor orientations situated center stage, the mouth should be the target. For orientations stage right, the left cheek should be the target. For orientations stage left, the right cheek should be the target. For proper placement have a colleague view the action to make sure that the fist is covering the target of the face for any given angle.

14.136

14.137

The Contact Punch

The main concepts and process used for executing this punch can be found in Chapter 13 Contact Violence. Playing the Floating Palm / Floating Fist game is a very good introduction to the technique for two performers who are getting used to contacting each other through strikes. The process outlined for the contact slap is a nearly identical process for the contact punch. The only difference here is that the punch never goes to the head but rather to one of the major muscle groups identified previously (abdominals, latissimus dorsi, etc.). Also, the operator uses a loose fist to make the contact instead of an open palm. All of the steps detailed for the contact slap should be repeated for the contact punch in order to explore the full possibilities of the technique. As always, the operator should focus on going to the target rather than through it. The more the body is animated and the hips are rotated during the action of the punch the more forceful the punch will look without actually transferring force into the target of the receiver. The reaction of the receiver should naturally be commensurate to the perceived force of the operator (Figures 14.138–14.141).

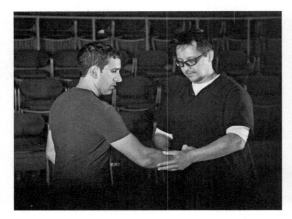

14.138

14.139

14.140

14.141

KICKS

Using the feet to strike can actually be a more common occurrence than one may think. Usually these attacks are ones of opportunity when the target we wish to attack is closer to the feet than any other part of the body. Kicking someone in the legs or while that person is on the ground can add an unexpected element to a scene of violence. Since the legs are larger limbs the perceived force transferred from the strike will seem greater to a viewing audience. However, because the legs are larger and most people outside of trained martial artists are not used to striking with the feet, extra practice and care must be taken with kicking techniques. The principles of distance, timing, and appropriate force must be in place for the kick to read and for the receiver to be comfortable in dealing with the blow.

For those performers with flexibility in the legs, any martial kick can be used to great effect on stage if the principles of both contact and non-contact violence are kept in mind. Roundhouse kicks, front kicks, hook kicks, wheel kicks, axe kicks, all are possible on stage. Since kicks require more space and more bodily movement to execute they can be wonderfully exciting theatrical techniques to employ, particularly in larger venues. The challenge becomes how does one justify the use of an axe kick in the context of a particular scene? It would make little sense for a character to throw a studied kick if there were no reference in either word or deed to the fact that the character has experience with such kicks. The use of these and any technique must be commensurate and logical in relation to the character, story, and style of the production.

It should be noted that for every kick it is important to *chamber* the kick before the knee before extending the leg (Figures 14.142 and 14.143). Chambering is the act of bending the leg at the knee before the leg is extended for the kick. This allows

14.142

14.143

for more control and precision of placement for the kick. It also helps with balancing on one leg for the duration of the kick. Additionally, any contact kick should be made using only the flattest surfaces on the foot or shoe. The tops of the laces or the flat of the sole are the most likely places to make contact for these kicks. However, with enough control and sensitivity to force, the instep and outside of the foot can be used as contact surfaces as well. As mentioned before, the types of kicks that end up having more utility in the context of the scene are those that target the lower extremities when the receiver is standing or on the ground. We will take a look first at those techniques that require contact between the operator and receiver and then adjust those techniques where contact does not occur.

Front Kick

14.144

This kick can be used in a variety of instances and orientations on stage. One of the most effective, however, is when the performers are in the operator upstage/receiver downstage offset position with the receiver facing upstage.

- If kicking with the right foot, the operator should line up in a slightly more offset position than the hand techniques to allow extra distance for the kick to develop.
- The operator chambers the knee straight up and in the direction of the intended target (Figure 14.145 – performance angle).
- As the operator chambers the knee, the receiver brings the hands well out in front of his or her body, into a variation of a shared knap: the cage knap. This knap is made by placing the hands flat (like karate chop hands) one on top of the other in a perpendicular orientation. The fingers of each hand should

14.145

be side by side and not loose or separated. The palms should be facing the incoming striking object (in this case the foot). This knap should be placed out in front of the receiver enough so that when the tops of the laces strike the hands there is enough clearance between the body of the receiver and the toe of the operator.

14.146

- The operator will extend the leg from the chambered position and strike the prepared cage-knapped hands of the receiver with the foot pointed. There should be a good solid sound to the shared knap upon contact.

- The operator returns through the chambered position to keep balance. Do not infringe on the receiver's reaction space.

- The most likely reaction of the receiver for this technique is to act as though he or she had been kicked in the gut or groin. If the receiver is slightly doubled over or kneeling to start and the operator has a flexible, high kick then this technique can also be sold as a kick to the face. Each of these reactions has distinct physical and vocal reactions for the receiver. The location of the strike and its effect should be carefully determined depending on the intended effect (Figures 14.144–14.148 – performance angle).

14.147

14.148

This kick can be easily converted to a non-contact technique by simply removing the cage knap. Of course, this deprives the technique of the actual sound of the foot striking a solid object. If, however, it is impossible to make the knap in this way then the receiver may execute either a body or vocal knap.

The front kick can also be used to great effect when the receiver is on the ground. Two such techniques target both the abdominals and groin respectively. Both of these techniques require contact and are typically used to end a confrontation and have a clear victor. To target both the abdominals and the groin follow the same process for making contact during a technique. It is important for the operator to remain balanced throughout the kick and to point the toes. Do not flex the foot (Figure 14.149) during these contact kicks as that will increase the likelihood of injury to both operator and receiver.

14.149

The body positions for the receiver on each of these techniques is very precise so as to minimize the chance for injury and also give the audience the best possible view of the power of the kick.

Abdominal Kick (on the Ground)

- The operator should find his or her distance to make sure that the tops of the laces contact the abdominals of the receiver in a place that is comfortable. Make sure that the location of the kick is placed squarely between the ribs and the hipbones on the abdominal sheath.

- The receiver should be positioned in such a way that the body is in an extended position supported by the arms and legs. Extending the body will elongate the abdominal sheath and create a larger target. Do not attempt this technique in a tabletop or hands-and-knees position. This position will increase the likelihood of making the spine concave and as a result bring the ribs and hipbones closer together. This increases the chance of hitting bone rather than muscle, which should be avoided at any cost.

- The body of the receiver should not be parallel or flat to the floor but rather lifted up from the floor with the body positioned at approximately a 45-degree angle towards the incoming foot of the operator. The exact angle should be judged by the operator so as to make the best fit for the foot to contact the stomach (Figure 14.155).

14.150

14.151

14.152

14.153

14.154

14.155

- If done right, there should be an appreciable sound upon contact between the shoe and the abdominals. After the sound of contact the receiver should make an appropriate vocalization while contracting the spine.
- Since this is a contact move the position can be in full view of the audience. The head of the receiver can be positioning either stage left or right. The operator may kick with whichever foot is more comfortable.

Groin Kick (on the Ground)

- The operator makes the same adjustments for distance, balance, foot position, and quality of contact as before.
- The receiver lies on his or her back with his or her head facing downstage towards the audience.
- As the operator comes forward the receiver initiates a slight back bridge by posting off of the upper back against the floor and lifting the hips off the floor to allow enough clearance for the operator's foot. This action should be done in time with the operator's approach as though the receiver were trying to get away from the kick when in fact the receiver is presenting the unobstructed target to the operator (Figures 14.156–14.158).

14.156, 14.157 & 14.158

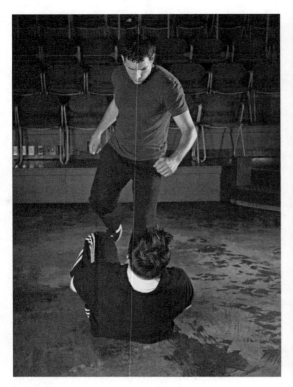

14.159

14.160

14.161

- The actual target for this technique is the gluteal muscles (Figure 14.161). Since the action of the kick usually wants to travel diagonally across the body the operator must be very precise with the tracking action of the kick. If the operator is right-footed then the target should be the right gluteal. If the operator is left-footed then the target should be the left gluteal. This specific targeting will minimize the foot from travelling to the sensitive area in the center of the hips.
- Once again, if performed well, there should be the sound of shoe on flesh upon contact. Then the receiver should make an appropriate vocalization and fold inward at the point of contact. The operator must make sure to retract the foot and leg completely from between the receiver's legs so as not to get the legs tangled during the reaction (Figures 14.159–14.160).

The Roundhouse Kick

The roundhouse kick also uses a chambering action, only this time the chamber happens with the knee pointing in towards the target and not straight up (Figure 14.162). The leg is then extended in such a way that the foot travels from the outside in towards the intended target (Figure 14.163). The motion is similar to the roundhouse punch described earlier.

14.162

14.163

14.164

14.165

14.166

While it may be possible for some flexible performers to kick high for this technique, the most useful targets to attack with this kick are the lower extremities. We can use our knowledge of contact hits to use the roundhouse kick to strike the back of the leg at the major muscle group of the hamstring.

- The operator should find a suitable distance where he or she can contact the hamstring of the receiver with the tops of the shoe at the laces. Make certain not to place the contact too close to the receiver's knee.
- When the proper distance is determined the roundhouse is performed with the chambering action described previously. Make certain that during the chamber the knee does not go past the line of the intended target. Positioning the knee past the line of the intended target increases the likelihood of the energy of the contact blow travelling through the target instead of to the target. At the moment of greatest extension for the leg the foot should just make enough contact with the hamstring to get a good sound but not transfer so much energy to the receiver that causes discomfort or damage.

- The contact should be made with the top of the laces while the foot is pointed.
- The receiver should react to this strike as though the initial damage was caused at the point of contact. A sharp, voluntary knee bend and pivot on the ball of the foot is a good way to accent the reaction to this strike (Figures 14.167–14.168). Oftentimes performers react to lower extremity strikes by moving the upper body or head first, which only distracts from the reality of the intended target and specificity of the moment.

14.167

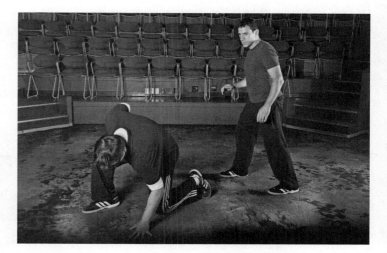

14.168

This type of kick is a useful technique to have at the ready especially when one character must be rendered slightly immobile or somehow be forced to the ground. For those performers with flexible kicks and more developed musculature it is possible to target different areas of the body such as the abdominals or the latissimus dorsi. Wherever the contact is made, be sure to follow the process of initiating contact for such a move. Communication between partners is essential to be in agreement about the precise target and quality of contact.

AVOIDANCES

So far all of the moments of violence we have examined have had intentions that have come to fruition. That is to say every violent instance has involved successfully realized actions. However, oftentimes most actions in a fight do not reach their intended target fully or at all. If the character receiving the violence is aware of what is happening then it makes sense he or she would do anything in his or her power to avoid that violence. The more invested the character is in avoiding the violence the higher the stakes will become for the scene. Additionally, by adding in avoidances we can create a feeling of uncertainty in the audience of not knowing when a certain given attack may be successful. As a result, the audience pays more attention to the conflict move by move.

In order to successfully avoid an incoming attack one thing must always be crystal clear: what is the intended target. Even if the performers know that a strike will not land they both must be invested enough in the action and the reaction so that the audience believes it would have landed had the receiver not moved out of the way. If this element is not firmly in place then the action of the operator and the reaction of the receiver will look disconnected and general.

Take, for example, a roundhouse punch to the face, or to be more exact, the left cheekbone (see Figures 14.169–14.171). The performers must establish a distance where it is likely that the operator could possibly strike the receiver after moving the whole body forward. Attacks that miss still require the operator to pursue the receiver. This gives the action a sense of

14.169

14.170

14.171

directed motion that obliges the receiver to move out of the way. If we recall from Chapter 3 Seeking Safety the principle of ARC (Action-Reaction-Completion) we find that the order of events outlined there provides us with a guide in sequencing this action in particular. The attack must happen first. The receiver then responds to the intent and physical nature of that attack with the appropriate reaction. Of course, if for whatever reason the receiver does not react by moving out of the way then the operator knows not to complete the action and put the receiver at risk. Once the receiver initiates the action then both operator and receiver can finish that particular moment by completing the ARC. The consequences of even a missed attack can be as terrifying as a successful one. Two characters who have had a loving relationship would have a tectonic shift to that relationship if one person started throwing fists at the other. That relationship will have changed irrevocably; nothing would be the same moving forward. Avoiding the danger allows the characters and the audience the opportunity to process violent intent in real time. Do not short shrift the importance and the power of these unsuccessful moves. Failure often reveals more about life than success.

Blocks

Responding to a character's intent regardless of whether violence is involved or not is of vital importance to any scene. It keeps the energy between the performers flowing in such a way that the audience knows exactly what is occurring moment by moment. Avoidances help engage with this element in performance quite well during moments of violence. Sometimes, however, the character cannot escape the path of an incoming attack fast enough to completely avoid it. In this instance the character must intercept the strike with a block to avoid the consequences of a more severe injury. Including blocks in a violent moment increases the chance of getting more theatrical mileage out of a moment as well. By showing that the performers are actually making contact with each other even in the form of the block the likelihood of the audience engaging with the physical reality of the moment is increased. Adding blocks gives the performers an opportunity to demonstrate the relative skill level of the characters they are playing. In the two techniques described below we will examine how to block with the upper extremities (arms and hands) to see how certain strikes can be blocked and how these blocks can denote a level of skill for the character. Since there is a quality of touch that must be adhered to for these blocks the guidelines for making contact outlined earlier should be followed for these techniques as well.

Palm Blocks

The palms of the hands are one of the most dramatically versatile and effective ways to block an incoming attack. Palm blocks are typically used for incoming punches but can be used to intercept kicks, elbows, and knees as well. The palms not only provide a flat surface to meet the strike, but also increase the possibility of getting sound from the block. This may be considered a shared knap but unlike the knaps detailed before this one does not simulate a hit resulting in damage. Both blocks will be of a roundhouse punch from different angles.

- The operator finds the appropriate distance where contact can actually occur between the performers and attacks with a roundhouse punch that swings in horizontally to the target of the receiver's chin. It is very important that the operator still tracks the strike to a specific target. This way even when the block is performed the audience can clearly see that the receiver would have been struck had the block not been successful (Figure 14.172).

14.172

- As the strike is moving towards the target the receiver should adjust his or her feet and hips in such a way to face the incoming strike. Movement of the feet away from the strike is preferable to allow the strike to develop and leave room for the block. Adding a slight avoidance also imbues the moment with more danger as it shows that the receiver is actually concerned about getting hit and does not take the block for granted (Figure 14.173).

14.173

- Do not anticipate the block. If the palms are placed in the spot to meet the block before the strike is even thrown the sequence of ARC is broken. The reaction cannot be complete before the action. They must meet in the same time signature together. Both performers are responsible for finding out exactly how this timing should be for a particular interaction.
- After the avoidance in the body and facing the strike, the receiver should raise the palms up to meet the incoming strike. The palms should be relaxed but not too cupped with the fingers pointed up. The optimal placement for the palms at the moment of contact is one hand at the middle of the forearm and one hand in the middle of the upper arm. If the operator has a long enough forearm then both palms could be placed at an equal spacing on the forearm. Avoid contacting the operator on the elbow as making contact on the joints should always be avoided (Figure 14.174).

14.174

- After the moment of contact has occurred both the attack and the block should be relaxed naturally so that the scene can continue. Try not to push the strike out of the way or grab the arm unless there is an express reason for it choreographically or in the context of the scene. Like strikes, blocks should not be lingered on but rather moved through to help connect action and reaction and create a through-line of intent for each character.
- To play with how different characters might respond one can differentiate the block gesturally. Very flat palms with a sharp movement might denote a more skilled or confident receiver. A larger movement of the arms with slightly more relaxed or "sloppy" hands might demonstrate a less skilled or more frightened receiver. Think of the block as a gesture and experiment with which the quality of block is right for the moment without sacrificing the technique.

Forearm Blocks

- The operator will find the appropriate distance for contact once again and attack with a roundhouse punch. This block most successful when meeting a roundhouse punch that is travelling at an angle on the downward diagonal. A good target for the operator would be the temple of the receiver. The block can also be used against an incoming horizontal roundhouse as well (Figure 14.175).

14.175

14.176

- As the attack moves forward the receiver should adjust the feet and hips to initiate a slight avoidance. By dropping the hips and moving the head away from the incoming strike the receiver will increase the perceived danger of the strike and also allow more space for the block to develop (Figure 14.176).
- The outside forearm of the receiver should meet the inside forearm of the operator at the point of greatest musculature for each. Make certain that the hands of each arm are positioned in such a way that the bones of the forearms do not collide (Figure 14.177).

14.177

- As always do not anticipate the block!
- Relax the arms after the block has occurred to move forward with the scene or to the next move.
- Blocks with the forearm will typically demonstrate that the receiver has more training as a fighter than the typical palm block. However, like any block, the forearm block can also be treated as a gesture to reveal something additional about the character. If the hand of the blocking arm is closed into a fist it may suggest that the character is blocking as a trained response and looking to punch back. If the hand of the blocking arm is open and extended it could suggest that the receiver is not as skilled and is blocking out of pure instinct.

PLAYING PAIN

Pain is never added to pain. It multiplies.

Anonymous

Regardless of technique, any violent moment will never be wholly woven into the fabric of the story if there is no reaction to the direct and immediate consequence of that action. Quite simply, someone must experience pain. Pain humanizes the characters. Of course, the magnitude of that pain is entirely dependent on the direction of the story and how that story changes as a result of the violence. One of the most egregious sins an actor can make in performing violence theatrically is not to react painfully to physical damage. If no pain is experienced after a moment of violence then the stakes of the scene diminish dramatically. If the actor does not engage with the experience of being hurt then there is no reason for anyone to expect that the audience will care about the well-being of the characters. The performers can only make the audience care by reacting truthfully to the violent circumstance and its consequences.

No matter what the nature of the violence breathing and vocal quality must be as carefully attended to in every aspect for volume, rhythm, and quality. This aspect of the work must be commensurate with the physical interaction between characters. Once the possible breath and vocalization are explored then the performer can start to more accurately and realistically communicate the one aspect of violence of which everyone has intimate knowledge: the knowledge of human suffering and pain.

Playing pain in performance is a tricky business. When in graduate school, two classmates of mine were rehearsing a scene where a young woman was attending the bedside of an old king who was sick. The scene was essentially about the young woman saying that she could heal the old king of his infirmity in exchange for some favor. My classmates seemed to miss their stride in the scene. There was no real reason for the old king who lay in bed to grant such favor to the young lady. Our teacher mentioned that since we could not see how much the king's infirmity affected him, there was no real need to listen to the young woman. They tried the scene again. This time the actor playing the old king was in an enormous amount of pain, wailing and screwing his face up on every other line to show how much pain he was in. This, however, did not improve the scene. Rather it presented a new problem. The scene became so much about the pain one character was experiencing that every other possible moment of connection between these two characters was lost. The pain trumped every other possible avenue of connection between the two characters.

Incorporating pain into a moment of violence in performance is absolutely necessary to make the audience care and believe that there is actually something at stake. Once proper vocalizations are explored as mentioned in the previous section based on location of the pain, then the performer can begin to further explore the exact quality of the pain. Quality of pain can be deduced if one knows the type of injury sustained. The following is a basic list of injuries that could be sustained in a violent unarmed altercation, which have distinct effects on the human body and therefore alter the quality of pain being experienced:

- *Crushing*. This type of damage causes bruising to soft tissue or muscle, breaking of bones, or even rupturing of organs if the blow is forceful enough. Think of the effect of a large hammer the size of a fist hitting any given area.
- *Penetrating*. This type of damage is invasive by breaking the skin and entering the body. The object tears and disrupts the internal structure upon entry. Think of a thumb being shoved and twisted into the eye socket.
- *Choking*. This type of damage specifically targets the systems that supply oxygen to the body. Typically the location of this kind of damage is targeted at the neck. Chokes can either deprive the receiver of oxygen by interrupting the exchange of air through crushing the trachea (windpipe) or interrupt the flow of oxygenated blood to the brain by collapsing the carotid arteries on the side of the neck.

Before the quality of the pain being experienced can be fully explored and expressed, two basic questions must be answered: what has injured me? And what type of injury from the above list does this object produce physiologically in the body? The games listed below help the performer answer such questions.

The Exotic Death Game or Circle of Destruction

This is a group game where the players all stand in a wide circle. There are no props to this game only the body and the imagination. One player begins by creating out of thin air a weapon of personal destruction. It could be anything – a knife, a sword, a rifle, a bazooka, an attack dog, a poison dart. But this weapon must be created using actions with the body and sound effects only. The player should not simply raise both arms and say, "It's a bazooka!" The player must act as though he or she had just locked and loaded a bazooka and is taking aim at a target. The target in this case is another player in the circle whom the player with the bazooka has chosen to destroy. The player with the weapon uses it in the way that particular weapon should be used (in this case, the bazookateer must launch the round toward the target). When the weapon is used on the player who is the receiver, that player must die in a fashion appropriate to being affected by that weapon. In the case of the bazooka, one or many limbs might be blown off from the torso. When the player experiences the trauma he or she must take a *full 20 seconds* to experience the particular pain of that trauma before expiring. This must be done outlandishly using the full limits of the body and the voice. On a reaction scale of 1–10 where 10 is the highest level, all of the death reactions should be at a 10. (It should be mentioned here that since this game relies on the players stretching their limits physically and vocally it should only be played after a thorough vocal and physical warm-up.) At about the 15-second mark, the player about to expire then creates his or her own weapon to use on another player. With the last ounce of strength, that player then targets another person in the circle who must go through the same throes of death and continue the circle of destruction. Once players have expired they should remain on the ground and observe the different and exotic items of destruction that are created and how each player responds to a particular weapon. The player who begins the game should be the last one to die.

This is a very fun game especially when the players try to out-imagine each other with ever increasingly outlandish weapons. (I once saw one player kill another with a pack of faeries. That's right. A pack of faeries. One of them was Tinkerbell.) Be sure not to short shrift the amount of time the players take to experience the pain of the trauma. Often players will want to scream once or twice and then create their weapon. If a player short changes his or her own agony the rest of the players should be encouraged to shout at that player "Keep dying!" to make sure the player investigates that particular trauma to its fullest vocally and physically.

The Pain Game

This game is an extension of the Circle of Destruction. The first time I ever played this game was at the Philly Cheesesteak Workshop in a class taught by SAFD Fight Master J. David Brimmer. It is a deceptively simple game but one that at the time opened my eyes to the reality that representing violence in performance is a necessary and practicable skill.

This game is best played after Circle of Destruction since that game is a good warm-up to the concepts of pain, death, and dying. It also introduces the concept of linking pain to the instrument that caused it. Start by throwing a small ball around the circle. Usually a tennis ball or any ball of comparable size and weight will do. The players can throw underhand or overhand as long as the ball reaches the target. After a few minutes when the group becomes comfortable throwing and receiving an object swap the tennis ball with a lacrosse ball. The size is roughly the same but the weight is very different. The introduction of a ball with more substantial weight should focus the group more to make good throws and catches. The players should find that it takes more full body attention to receive the energy of the lacrosse ball. After a few minutes with the lacrosse ball put the ball down but continue throwing the ball as if it were there. This imaginary ball should be thrown in the same way as the lacrosse ball with the throwers putting effort into accurate throws and the catchers putting their whole body into receiving the energy of the toss.

After a few more moments of this pass-around with the imaginary ball, the nature of the ball changes. The ball becomes like a lead shot put. Except this shot put is very special. It has infinite mass. It is the heaviest, densest object in the universe. This would naturally mean that no one could lift it. But now in the game every player has developed infinite strength. So everyone can now pick up and throw the ball. However, there is one problem. No one is invincible. So now when the players with infinite strength throw the ball with infinite mass it travels so fast that no one can catch it. So the ball ends up doing damage to wherever it happens to strike the receiver. The game begins in the same way as Circle of Destruction with one player throwing the ball, in this case the weapon, towards a very specific location on the body of another player standing in the circle. The location of the damage will be dictated by the aim and eye focus of the player throwing the ball. The damage done to the receiver is blunt force trauma. Crushing damage. When a player is struck, he or she will experience the pain caused by the damage physically and vocally for a *full 30 seconds*. The scale here varies slightly from Circle of Destruction in that the pain here may ebb and flow depending on the damage caused. However, even though the range of the pain experienced has increased, the players should nonetheless still be investigating the physical, emotional, and psychological pain produced by the damage fully and deeply through their inner and outer senses.

If possible, the instructor or knowledgeable member of the group can side coach the player experiencing the pain about what physiologically may be happening depending on the location of the trauma. For example, if a player has been struck in the shoulder I may say that the shoulder has been dislocated and needs to be put back in the socket. I will describe the ligaments tearing on the inside causing such pain that any movement of that arm is impossible. Then I'll ask if the person writes with that hand. If the answer is yes then I will suggest that it might not be possible to use that arm ever again and that all of the skills that person was good at with that arm must now be relearned with the other arm. Another example might be trauma to the torso. I may suggest that the strike has caused a pneumothorax and that the lung is collapsing and that it is more and more difficult to breathe. I may complicate this by saying that the ribs have also been broken and that one of the fractured ribs has punctured the lung and the lung is now filling up with blood. These images, while unsettling, are useful in giving the players concrete images of what could be happening to their physical bodies as a result of a specific trauma. This takes what was a general notion of pain and focuses their experience to a specific physical response.

The physical images may bring up emotional or psychological responses as well when they investigate the severity of the trauma and the possible imagined consequences. It should be suggested that the damage caused might affect the player's ability to operate normally on a daily basis, or prohibit advancement in a certain profession because of a new physical handicap, or even change the player's relationship to a loved one because of a disfigurement. Not everyone in the group need go through the same checklist of elements to consider. But all should be considered as possible when addressing the consequences of a specific injury and the particular pain associated with it. This will give the group a wide variety of experiences on which to draw.

Another element of this game to consider is the role of the other players who are witnessing a particular player actively experiencing the pain caused by the particular damage done. This aspect of the game is very important to consider for two reasons. First, it gives the other players an idea of how they may react physically and emotionally when playing a character who must witness the pain or death of another character. And second, it also gives the group a sense of how an audience may respond to viewing another human being in pain or about to die. This kind of information is vitally important to any performer. A scene where a character experiences pain or is about to die is probably the most intimate moments of a character's journey in the course of a play. How that character responds to hardship, pain, or the end of life is the kind of stuff that people pay to see in performance. Giving a moment like that short shrift denies the performer and the audience of what should be a moment that is full, vital, and human. Investigating how observers respond to moments like these will inform an actor's choices for how he or she approaches this aspect of the work.

Finally, it should be said that after the game is played the players will feel spent. This game tends to cause physical and emotional exhaustion for some more than others. Make sure to leave some time, at least 10 minutes, for a debriefing session where everyone can talk freely about what sensations, emotions, desires, and images they experienced during the game.

There are two very simple guidelines to follow when responding to an injury in performance that can show the audience exactly where the character has been hurt.

- *Touch the location of the pain.* This should be apparent to anyone who has received an injury however insignificant. When the body recognizes pain the hands typically seek out the location as quickly as possible. The hands hold on to the body part, rub it, and prod it. The hands get as much information as possible about the extent of the injury, especially if the injury is not immediately visible. If the hurt is extensive the hands will want to hold on to the affected area for a longer duration if possible. This is the body's way to apply pressure to an injury. This also provides a quick remedy to help reduce swelling at the site of the injury.
- *Wrap the body around the pain.* This idea may be a little odd in the phrasing. It is not that the body is actually attempting to embrace the pain physically (unless that is a particular character choice). Rather, the body attempts to isolate the source of the pain by removing the precise area that is struck. This is not dissimilar to the body's reaction to an incoming threat. In order not to be injured the body would remove the threatened target. Even though the injury occurs after the body can successfully remove the target from danger, the mechanics are the same. If one were to imagine a ball the size of the imagined injury, the performer should attempt to curve the body in some way around that space while removing the rest of the body as far from that space as possible. The performer can accentuate this movement with good limb and joint articulation, particularly with the spine. If one thinks of a punch to the stomach, the most appropriate reaction would be to contract the abdominals and curve the spine around that trauma. This particular instance involves a curvature of the spine in a specific region relative to the location of the blow. It is not a general reaction of bending at the waist and doubling over. That is far too general of a reaction for any injury to the midsection. Also, the act of doubling over and looking at the floor deprives the audience of a clear view of the performer's face. For storytelling and character purposes, the head should remain up with the face visible. This will allow the performer to clearly express how the character feels about that injury in the moment to the audience and to any other characters who may witness the injury – particularly the character that just inflicted the damage!

Discovering the quality and effect of pain on the human body for every possible circumstance is an indispensable component of the art of unarmed stage combat. Without it the actors cease to be characters that can be changed and affected by actions. Rather, they become performers who are demonstrating a physical routine with some sounds after which everyone will get back to the business of the rest of the play. Nothing can more quickly take an audience out of the transporting nature of theatre or cinema than a performer who is unaffected by things that happen to him or her in during the course of the story. By being bold, differentiating, and exact in the presentation of pain during moments of violence the performer can exploit yet another avenue to vitally connect with an audience. Don't miss that opportunity.

For videos demonstrating the techniques from this chapter, please visit the companion website at www.focalpress.com/cw/najarian or scan the following code:

Final Thoughts

Acting is easy. Anyone can get up in front of a group of people and pretend to be something they are not. People do this every day to one degree or another. Most use these masks to hide their true feelings or intentions rather than reveal something about themselves or the world. Stage combat is easy. Anyone can swing arms and legs at another person. Anyone can pretend to be hurt. People do this all the time too. They flail about their lives undirected towards any particular intention or goal. They feign frailties because they are afraid of attempting to do something and looking like a fool. Or worse, they are afraid to unleash a source of power within themselves they dare not acknowledge. Better never to try and create a certainty of avoiding disappointment or elevation to a state that we fear to achieve.

To act well is difficult. Everyone participates in the same game of acting but some people are better at the game than others. They believe they are the thing they present with more conviction and certainty. When they believe it more then we believe it more. They engage with their inner narrative in such a way that it becomes real to them. With enough conviction it begins to become real to anyone observing. To perform violence believably on stage is tough. It may be the toughest part of the craft. The physical and emotional requirements are staggeringly risky for the performer. If any part of the moment is not known down to the smallest detail then there is the possibility for actors to be injured and for skepticism and incredulity on the part of the audience. The stakes are so high and yet we often fail at consistently hitting the mark of truly affecting an audience by revealing the terrible ways in which the members of humanity bring violence to bear on one another.

All too often a moment of violence in a play is never fully explored. Rather, it is managed. The producer, director, and actors due to lack of skill, imagination, forethought, and time want to have a simple, one-size-fits-all technique to insert into the particular moment so that the show can resume with the more strongly interpreted points of the play. If there is any moment of a play to be strongly presented it is the moment of violence where the relationships between characters change irrevocably. The true nature of violence is as particular as you can get since it depends on the exact nature of the interaction. A beating is very different from a strangling. A man hitting a woman conjures very different feelings than a woman hitting a man. Violence demands that we pay close attention to the quality of interaction and relationship. To gloss over this does a disservice to the creative process and robs an audience of a full experience. The art form should not be generalized and diluted to fit the capabilities of the actors; actors must rise to the level of the work in order to make the art complete.

Stage combat is the expression of character through violent, combative form. The aim is to combine natural instinct and physical control within and between performers. Performers usually speak of instincts and impulses. These are things to follow and honor and not impede. If those impulses are not given an exact form then there is no way to affect anything outside of the performer. If only physical control exists then the performer merely discharges a set of actions. The goal of theatre is to combine these elements to have a specific and purposeful effect on our partners, then the audience, and then the world. Natural instinct in the extreme is feral and not part of society. Physical control in the extreme creates an automaton. The harmony of the two becomes art.

Sources, Bibliography, and Suggested Reading

HISTORY OF STAGE COMBAT

Wikipedia: http://en.wikipedia.org/wiki/Stage_combat

Martinez, J.D. 1996 *The Swords of Shakespeare*. McFarland & Company Inc., Jefferson, NC.

Nevitt, Lucy 2013 *Theatre & Violence*. Palgrave Macmillan, New York.

HOPLOLOGY

Wikipedia: http://en.wikipedia.org/wiki/Hoplology

Wise, Arthur 1971 *The History and Art of Personal Combat*. Hugh Evelyn, London.

Miller, Rory 2008 *Meditations on Violence*. YMAA Publication Center, Boston, MA.

GOOD PARTNERING: COOPERATION VS. COMPETITION

Gallwey, W. Timothy 1974 *The Inner Game of Tennis*. Random House Trade Paperbacks, New York.

TRAINING

Dintiman, George B., Ward, Robert D., Tellez, Tom 1997 *Sports Speed*. Human Kinetics, Champaign, IL.

Gelb, Michael 1981 *Body Learning*. Henry Holt and Company, New York.

Pearlan, Steven J. 2006 *The Book of Martial Power*. The Overlook Press, Woodstock, NY.

CHARACTERS IN CONFLICT

Stanislavski, Constantin 2003 *An Actor Prepares.* Routledge, New York.

Donnellan, Declan 2002 *The Actor and the Target.* Theatre Communications Group, St. Paul, MN.

NON-CONTACT VIOLENCE

Wikipedia: http://en.wikipedia.org/wiki/Isometric_exercise

SEEKING SAFETY

Girard, Dale 1997 *Actors on Guard.* Routledge, New York.

GAMES

Barker, Clive 1977 *Theatre Games.* Drama Book Specialists, New York.

VIOLENT SOUNDSCAPE

Linklater, Kristin 1976 *Freeing the Natural Voice.* Drama Publishers, New York.

Huxley, Aldous 1982 *The Art of Seeing.* Creative Arts Book Company, Berkeley, CA.

VASTA and Dal Vera, Rocco (ed.) 2001 *The Voice in Violence.* Voice and Speech Trainers Association, Inc. Cincinnati, OH.

TECHNIQUES

Howell, Jonathan 2008 *Stage Fighting: A Practical Guide.* Crowwood Press, Wiltshire, UK.

Suddeth, J. Allen 1996 *Fight Directing For the Theatre.* Heinemann, Portsmouth, NH.

Lane, Richard 1999 *Swashbuckling.* Limelight, Pompton Plains, NJ.

Index